Natal

Steven Cavini

Natalia

Her life, her family, her tragedy

Natalia: Her life, her family, her tragedy
ISBN 978 1 76109 345 6
Copyright © text Steven Cavini 2022

First published 2022 by
GINNINDERRA PRESS
PO Box 3461 Port Adelaide 5015
www.ginninderrapress.com.au

Dedicated to Adriana, Jason and Natalie

Foreword

Why did I write this book?

It is a story worth telling, in the general sense that I believe everyone's story is worth telling, but also, specifically, it is the story of my mother and her family, a migrant family. It explores some aspects of her early life in Italy, the beginnings of her own family and the details behind their decision to migrate to Australia, beyond the clichéd theme of the 'search for a better life'. Life, as in Natalia's case, is more complex than that. I look at what happened to their dreams and the tragedy, with respect to chronic illness, that befell her, with the enormous toll that severe illness took on the sufferer as well as the family.

Her illness has given me a certain outlook on life which has endured and even strengthened over time. It is perhaps her most important legacy, other than the genes she has passed on. It has given me strength. I find, when subjected to life's grinding tumults, that the coming to mind of what my mother endured reduces the significance of my own pains. This may not be a healthy way of looking at things but it is an automatic pattern of thought that she has left me with, as all parents pass things on to their children, whether intentionally or unintentionally.

She has given me strength to endure many tribulations and an undying attitude to get on with the job and not make excuses. Above all, she has taught me to treasure good health, as all should, for it is mostly taken for granted and can be snatched away in a moment.

This biography is as factual as I can make it. However, there are some scenes and sections of dialogue where I have used creative licence and imagined how things may have occurred.

I hope that my humble work is of interest to some.

1

Photos lie. They always have and always will, nowadays more than ever before. It is an art, for want of a better word, as rooted in deception as the trickery of the magician or the guile of the fake healer. Smoke and mirrors; mirrors and smoke. The very nature of the pose is a distortion of reality, every bit as distorted as that of an object when seen through a nest of prisms.

We look at an idealised photo of a family, together and smiling, and invariably say what a wonderful or beautiful family, reflecting the paradigm of the idyllic essence of family cohesion. But in many cases there is falsity there: forced smiles, unwelcome embraces, strained union. It may well be that the sole bond is familial and, but for that, the varied parts would spring apart like magnets of similar poles.

Likewise, in a glamorous portrait photo, we say how beautiful a woman looks or how handsome a man looks when they have been specifically altered for the occasion to the point of being barely recognisable from their day-to-day selves. A photo may deliberately portray strength where there is only weakness, or gentleness where the brutal characteristics of Homo sapiens lurk just below the surface.

The point is that they have all been altered to achieve some sort of potential or desirable image, but what is the reality? Photos rarely tell us. They squirt untruths like shit from a goose; easily, seamlessly, effortlessly. They spill half-truths surreptitiously and with the hypnotic charm of a snake. They are virtually incapable of portraying truth unless done candidly.

These are the dark, tarnished thoughts I have now as I hold a photo that was taken back in 1955, four years before I was born. It is framed, black and white, and hangs permanently in my lounge room. Until recently, it has always been a favourite of mine but now I have slowly and bitterly come to the realisation that I was duped and that it has taken almost sixty years for me to realise it.

As seen on the cover of this book, it depicts my father, mother and sister walking along a pier in the port of Trieste, about to board the *Flaminia* for their journey to Australia. I've looked at it a thousand times but never really seen its detail.

My mother, Natalia, is on the left. In her right hand she holds a large bunch of flowers given to her by her family; in her left is a travel bag.

In the middle is my sister, Adriana, or Adi for short; nine years old at the time. She has a handbag slung over one shoulder and the family camera slung over the other and she is clutching a piece of paper in both hands, which I assume is her ticket to a strange new land. I can imagine the excitement it gave her; she had a bag she could have put it into but simply couldn't bear to let it go.

My father, Guido, is on the right. He holds a parcel tied with string in his left hand that contains Adi's favourite doll; his right hand is un-encumbered and appears to swing freely and I realise for the first time that it is the only hand of six to have that luxury and that, oddly enough, it is absolutely symbolic of his carefree and unencumbered at-titude to life.

In the background is a majestic building with formal columns, part of the stunning Austrian architecture of Trieste, and the ship.

This photo has always been important to me. In an instant, it has captured who I am; my origins. It moves me deeply, more than I can really say. That day is a sunny July day in Trieste, the sort of day that lifts one's spirits. Their stride is purposeful. My father looks straight ahead, my mother and sister look at the camera. It portrays confidence, optimism, decisiveness, unity and strength of purpose. Three people striding forward as one to fulfil their dreams in a new land. It speaks of a solid grounding, unshakable faith and unbreakable unity. It is also a complete fabrication. That is no easy thing to say about your own family but there you have it; I've said it.

My mother is positioned at the centre of the photo and it is to her that I am mainly drawn. Her image still surprises me after all this time. It is of a woman I don't know; a woman before my time. She looks so young, beautiful and incredibly healthy. Her hair is dark and tidy and her dress, which she would have made herself, is elegant and extends down to calf level. She looks intently at the camera with a serious expression that seems to dare the photographer to ask her to smile. I can't believe that this is the same mother that I knew and that I experienced, albeit after her world had been torn apart. There is nothing in the photo that portends what was to come. Quite the opposite, in fact. Its undeniable message is that they are confidently about to leave for another country halfway around the world to live happily ever after come what may. It has no prognostic value whatsoever.

My father looks a little odd, perhaps uncomfortable in his jacket with the heat. There is a sheen to his forehead, the top button of his shirt is undone and he is not wearing a tie. He is a little separate from wife and daughter. He has what seems to me to be a forced, half-smile of impatience. He looks like a man who has just had an argument with his wife, is trying to put it behind him and simply wants to get the show on the road. He is a man I don't know, also from another age, at odds with the man I got to really know in only the last few years of his life.

My sister is the only one of those three people on the pier at that time that I can say I know. I know her well, we are close, even though we rarely meet. We have the enduring bond that goes with being siblings, forged from shared experiences, good and bad. In my own inadequate way, I love her, and if she goes before me, I will miss her.

Below the photo, within the same frame, is a short piece of prose I wrote to go with it. It's a nice little piece but, just like the photo, it is not entirely accurate. I had entered it into a writing competition and took some liberties with the story so as to fit in more with the theme of the competition, which was 'Preservation', but now it seems quite apt and entirely consistent with the liberties taken with the construction of the photo itself.

So, enough about the photo, I've had my fill of it and it will be some time before I feel the need to look at it again. At the moment, I hate it and would happily never look at it again, but that feeling will pass as feelings invariably do with time. Now, the time has come to return it to its place on the wall and to focus instead on the story which pre- and post-dates it.

2

Natalia Regent, my mother, was born in Contovello on 20 March 1921. It was then a small village on the karst plateau a short distance inland from Trieste, of which it is now a suburb. Back then, it was a rural community set amongst beautiful forested hills, noted in particular for its viticulture, and a stone's throw from another village, Prosecco. Its smattering of dwellings surrounded the Church of San Girolamo, like obedient stationary planets around a gloriously nurturing sun. In common with all Italian villages at the time, the church was the epicentre of community life, worship and education.

The inhabitants were mostly Slavs. My mother spoke mostly Slovenian at home, with some Italian thrown in, and learned Italian at school. She was fluent in both languages as well as being quite proficient in German. Before the end of the First World War, Trieste was part of the Austro-Hungarian empire and prospered, as the empire's major port, to become a critical commercial hub and its fourth largest city. A railway linked it directly with Vienna, making the city on the Adriatic a very popular tourist destination also. The stunning Austrian architecture has left a legacy which to this day gives Trieste a different feel to other Italian cities.

In the carve-up of territory which followed the First World War, Trieste became part of the kingdom of Italy, but Italy's territorial gains had come at a frightfully high price, paid in blood and misery, in the battle lines of the Alps and at the twelve battles on the Isonzo river, including the shambolic rout at Caporetto.

Natalia was born into a post-war maelstrom of poverty, bitterness, anti-Slovak tension, forced Italianisation and the first appearance on the world stage of Fascism. It was a time of immense struggle and hardship, shortages of everything and, for many people, hunger and famine. The privations of this generation, forced on them by war, produced in them an almost fanatical stoicism and pride, the esteemed values of family life and hard work, immense appreciation of simple things, intense dislike and suspicion of the well-to-do who were considered to be greedy, selfish capitalists or war profiteers, and disdain for those that did not grasp opportunity with both hands.

A common mantra at the time was *prima i doveri, dopo i diritti*, first duties, then rights. For most adults at the time, there were few rights; for most children, there were virtually none. As the second of five children, and the oldest female, Natalia was forced to finish school at the end of grade four to help her mother with the domestic tasks. For a bright girl who loved school, this was an exceedingly bitter pill, but one that had to be swallowed by many children at the time.

Very few went on to secondary or more advanced education. It was a luxury few could afford. Those who did were usually bright boys who managed to gain a scholarship. As children, you put up, you endured, you did what you had to do, you did as you were told and you certainly didn't answer back or show any disrespect. Praise was scarce and had to be earned the hard way and, when simply getting by was a day-to-day struggle, the sensibilities of children amounted to nothing. They in turn became tough resilient adults, uneducated but clever, willing to forge ahead no matter what, without an overbearing sense of entitlement, and willing to put in the hard work required without complaint. Almost universally, they wanted better for their children, but for many there was always a deep sense of loss, of a life unlived, of opportunity denied, of something stolen from them; and a propensity for cruelty.

The sacrificial slaying of her education on the altar of duty to family filled Natalia with resentment she carried for the rest of her life. Her schoolbooks were used to light the fire for cooking and heating. She cooked, cleaned, got the younger children ready for school and helped with the plot of land which was their main source of food and their salvation. Her skill and creativity with needle and thread became legendary within the family. She was said to have *'mani di fata'*, the hands of a fairy. She mended old clothes, created new ones with whatever material was at hand, as if by divine miracle, and even became accomplished at making shoes for the family. It was a talent which in time would blossom into a fulfilling career, only to be cruelly cut short.

It was a time when land was everything. To have a plot of land in the country meant the difference between hunger and relative satiety. City dwellers often had it much tougher unless they were fortunate enough to have well paid employment. With land, there was always some fruit and vegetables, chickens, eggs and a pig or two to stave off the vicious pangs of an empty stomach. Natalia helped with the growing and harvesting of fresh produce, preserving food, as well as helping her mother, Luigia, with her weekly market in Ponte Rosso; selling their fresh produce, flowers and some fish to supplement the family income. The fish were caught by Natalia's father, Giovanni, and her eldest brother Mario.

Giovanni was Slovenian with Austrian ancestry and had fought with Austria in the war. After the war, he had a secure but low-paid job as a municipal clerk in Trieste. He did some fishing on the side to top up the funds but much of it, unfortunately, went straight to the bottle.

Having somehow endured the unendurable nightmare of war, none were unscathed, and the armies which had fought on the Italo-Austrian front became an army of drunks. Most paydays, Giovanni would come home obliterated, belligerent but also temporarily unburdened of the recurring thoughts and nightmares of that conflict. The war had moved from the valleys and mountains to the family home, where armistices and treaties were not to be found. Luigia, hard as nails and scant of compassion, took not one step back and gave as good as she got.

There are very few photos of any of my grandparents. I have seen a photo of Giovanni when he was older. He has a stern face and a down-turned mouth that make it hard to believe he could ever break into a smile; and yet, if one of my uncles is to be believed, he was fundamentally a good and decent man tormented by a cold, bossy wife. Rather

Natalia's mother Luigia,
date unknown.

Natalia's father Giovanni,
date unknown.

than a cruel face, it is perhaps the face of a disappointed man who has always found love and warmth beyond his reach, and of a man deserving of compassion and understanding who has gained neither.

Mario, whom Natalia adored, also finished school after grade four and helped his father to fish and do other odd jobs. As he got older, he fought with his father more and more when he intervened on his mother's side to protect her. The fights between father and son were ugly, physical and increasingly brutal, stoked, no doubt, by the festering resentment between father and mother. On one occasion at the end of a fight, Mario was left dangling, battered and bruised, on a butcher's hook, like a piece of meat. It was a vicious act to inflict on a child and nowadays it is difficult to conceive that such brutality could occur between parent and child but in a brutal era after a brutal war such acts were not far from the norm and often seen as necessary in preparing children, toughening them up, for the brutal world at large. Soft children wouldn't survive. Soft children would be a burden. Resilience was paramount.

The violence escalated as Mario got older and, inevitably, matters came to a head when Natalia was only ten years old.

3

'Peel the potatoes, Dali [Natalia's family nickname]. And make sure you wash them properly. I don't want grit in the soup,' Natalia's mother barked.

When alight, the wood stove was a living thing, a pumping heart pulsating the kitchen with its warmth and utility and becoming the focus of all activity, just like the belle of the ball.

Luigia threw a few more pieces of wood into the firebox, then stirred the pot of barley, beans and sauerkraut that simmered on the cooktop. Mother and eldest daughter were making *jota*, a traditional hearty soup of the region, to be had with a piece of the bread that was just forming a lovely crust in the oven. All the ingredients were their own except for the barley, which they procured by bartering fish they had caught. Sauerkraut was made from their own cabbage. The beans, potatoes and garlic were all home-grown. On this occasion, they even had a small piece of smoked hock, from the last pig Giovanni had butchered, which gave the soup a delightful flavour.

The smell in the tiny kitchen, of the soup and the baking bread, was wondrous and would remain a cherished memory, intensely nostalgic, to Natalia's dying day. As long as Natalia could cook, *jota* would remain a family staple.

'Quickly, Natalia! Mario will be home soon, with a good catch if God wants it so.'

Natalia remained silent. She knew Mario would be home soon and she was already working quickly as a result. She also knew that Mario had a special status with her mother that required his meals to be ready on time, for he was the eldest son and he worked very hard. So all these orders that her mother was issuing to her were totally superfluous. She knew exactly what to do and always performed her tasks well. It was important for her to do so not just to avoid a scolding but also to enhance her own pride but, she thought wearily, for some reason it seemed important to her mother to bark the orders at her. She knew not why. Luigia did the same to her husband, until his tolerance would crack and his cool would be lost, then she would back off for a short period. She also did the same to her other daughters, Aniça (pronounced Anitsa) and Nina, although, Natalia noticed, not to the same extent, because they were younger.

To Mario, there was no snapping of orders at all. Rather, they took the form of polite and at times almost reverential requests, which he could refuse without repercussion, although he rarely did so. And to Giuseppe, the youngest, the baby, the golden boy, there were no orders or requests at all, only praise, and encouragement to do well at school. In fact, Giuseppe

Natalia's confirmation, circa 1931 with her godmother (name unknown).

was the only one of the five to complete an education. He finished primary school, attended technical school and became an electrician.

Natalia understood that self-sacrifice was the natural lot to befall the eldest daughter, but nevertheless it was another cause for the deep, multi-pronged resentment which she forever carried. She didn't like injustice, she loathed unfairness, and her bitterness remained from that time on for the rest of her life, as did her dislike of Giuseppe because of the privilege he'd received. She considered him spoilt and selfish, exemplified by the fact that he remained living in the family home, as if a birthright, for the rest of his life without ever sharing it with his siblings or buying them out.

They were making a large pot of *jota*, enough for tonight and also for tomorrow night, when it would taste even better. Luigia continued to stir with a large wooden spoon lest the bottom of the thick soup

Three of Natalia's siblings. From left, Nina, Peple and Aniça.

should burn and taint the soup with a burnt flavour. Drops of soup spattered onto the hotplate, adding a not unpleasant smell of burning juices to the air. Natalia placed the spotless diced potatoes into the pot then, seeing that the bread was ready, removed it from the oven before being told to do so. Luiga checked it to make sure that it was to her satisfaction but said nothing. It was a small victory for Natalia.

'Did you add salt?'

'Yes, Mamma.'

'And pepper?'

'Yes, Mamma.'

Luigia skimmed a little fluid from the top of the soup and tasted it to make sure. Natalia always wondered why her mother bothered to ask but it seemed to be more a ritual than a wilful act of distrust. She used the robust wooden spoon that had probably been in the family for a hundred years and that, aside from its usefulness with cooking, had also connected with generations of backsides on innumerable occasions. Its construction and sting were known to be as formidable as its owner's.

Luigia placed a lid on the pot with a grudging humph to indicate her satisfaction with the level of salinity and pepperiness. Natalia, having removed the bread from the oven and placed it on a cooling rack, returned the thick rag which was used for that purpose back to its hook near the stove, it being the place of its lodging for as long as Natalia could remember; never washed, never replaced.

It was a heavy rye loaf, very hearty. Natalia had heard that for some reason wheat flour was scarce at the moment. No matter, rye flour was more than adequate and better than buckwheat. The look of its dark crust and the smell it gave off filled her mouth with juices and made her stomach get on its knees and beg.

The spell created by the hot loaf was broken by the sound of footsteps and banging metal buckets at the front door. It was Mario, the quiet, dutiful son; respectful, warm and affectionate; the provider who, even at the age of twelve, expected nothing more than a meal in return; and his mother's saviour and protector and perhaps the only thing that gave her life any meaning and a reason to persist and endure; a surrogate husband and father in all respects bar one. The effect on Luigia was as if all the bells of San Girolamo were pealing in all their glory to proclaim the second coming. She quickly wiped her forged hands on her apron and rushed to the door to welcome him but also, in a more practical sense, to inspect the catch of the day and in so doing immediately gauge the level of their short-term prosperity.

The greeting was one that Natalia never experienced. It is the greeting that a proud mother reserves for the much-loved eldest son who has not disappointed and, by virtue of which, in her mind at least, places him in the de facto position as head of the family.

'*Guarda che bravo! Mio amore!*' a love-struck Luigia bellowed.

He had barely time to rest his fishing rods against the rock wall of the house and set his buckets down before Luigia cupped his face in both her hands and kissed each cheek and, although he protested against all the fuss, Natalia knew that in a harsh, thankless world, this show of affection sustained him. He was the heroic warrior returned from battle, the noble hunter, the selfless provider; bound by duty, not acclaim.

The buckets were full of mullet, calamari and even a large octopus. For now, they would eat very well indeed and even make some money at the market. He went off to clean and fillet the fish and put them in salt, without being ordered to do so. The guts would be fed to the pigs and the heads and bones would be used to make a fish stock for soup or risotto. Nothing was wasted. All the while, Natalia continued to stir the large pot of *jota* in silence.

Natalia was happy when Mario came home and they were together again and she was glad that he had had a good catch. She loved Mario very much. He was her favourite, and a good elder brother. She understood that the bringing of food was more important than its cooking and delicately accepted that her role was a lesser one. She felt no ill will towards Mario for the fact that her role was undervalued, it was not his fault and he certainly did nothing to encourage it. His nature was warm and his spirit generous and he possessed not the slightest streak of meanness. It was just the way it was, the natural order of things as decreed by Luigia and the times, but the hurt was there and it festered deep within. Her work and sacrifice was always secondary, unappreciated, unacknowledged and perpetual.

The mother sat with her five children to eat. The *jota* steamed in their bowls and the bread was ripped apart. The wooden spoon was never far away to enforce proper manners and silence. As it was payday, they didn't wait for father to come home before starting. He could be home at any hour but most likely after closing time at the local *osteria*, and it was most unlikely that he would be in any state to eat. In any case, if he was hungry, he could serve himself and serve him right.

After dinner, they remained in the kitchen where it was warm and busied themselves in various ways. The daughters tidied up. Luigia, exhausted now, sat with her knitting and a cup of ersatz coffee with chicory. Mario tended to his fishing rods; untangling line, cleaning reels and sharpening hooks. Giuseppe read a book. None of them were musical, more's the pity, and there was no radio to pass the hours.

Natalia was the frailest of the three girls, pale and physically weaker. She retired to a chair to mend a pair of Giuseppe's pants for school the next day. Nina, physically strong, cleared the kitchen and swept the floor. She was never one of Natalia's favourites because of her frivolity, preference for menial tasks and dislike of school. After completing her tasks, Nina wanted to play cards but no one took her up on the offer. Natalia loved her third sister, Aniça, as much as she loved Mario, for her intelligence and capacity for serious conversation. She too was denied the immense benefit of further education and was to devote her life to one man and their children.

To an outsider, the family together in the bosom of the warm kitchen, each occupied in their own way in symbiotic kinship, would seem idyllic. The lanterns provided a beacon of soft light as the dark cold world seeped into everything else. But to those within, the warmth and peace papered over the chill tension that went with waiting for Giovanni's arrival. The wife and mother, well aware of the effects that alco-

Natalia, circa 1935.

hol and much talk of unworthy spouses and ungrateful children would
have on his mood, braced herself.

The haphazard stomp and shuffle of feet, like a flat fanfare, announced Giovanni's homecoming. He swore in slurred tones as he
tripped over Mario's fishing rods and muttered something to the effect
that they were a danger and should have been put away. Everyone
stopped what they were doing and waited. He had arrived earlier than
usual, a point not lost on Luigia, and as he entered, she immediately
went on the offensive out of complete disdain of drunkenness.

'Kick you out early did they?' she asked, not looking up.

'Don't start, you bitch. They don't kick me out. I leave when I'm
good and ready.'

'Don't speak like that in front of the children!'

'It's my house and I'll speak any damn way I like.' He reeled and belched and for a moment they thought he might throw up right there on the kitchen floor. 'In f…front of the children or not…in front of the children. I don't care. It's…it's all the same to me. Now get me some dinner.'

Luigia did not move any muscles other than those already in use for breathing, knitting and sipping coffee. She ignored him completely. Everyone knew there would be consequences and with the escalating tension there seemed to be a slowing of time, as if obeying some law of relativity, that focused attention and heightened the drama. Giovanni took a menacing step forward and staggered towards Luigia and as a result Mario put down his fishing line and prepared himself with deep breaths and taut muscles.

'I said I want some dinner,' he said, ominously.

'It's there, on the stove, waiting for you, and there's some bread on the table. Help yourself. I'm not your slave.'

'You heartless cow. I work my arse off all day to provide for you lot, my family, and this is the thanks I get.'

'I'm too busy with stomachs to worry about hearts. Get it yourself or go hungry.'

Luigia had a sharp tongue and was liberal with it. It got her into a lot of trouble with Giovanni, as well as others in the town, but she didn't seem to care. Rather, she seemed to welcome it. Natalia thought of her mother as hard and totally fearless but her recklessness worried her. She had often seen first-hand what her total disregard for diplomacy could do and what worried her even more of late was that Mario seemed to bear the consequences of her intransigence more and more in his efforts to defend her. Natalia couldn't recall a happy moment between mother and father, only spite; and it was getting worse. In the naïve eyes of a ten-year-old, she saw nothing between them that could in any way be described as love and yet she knew that her father was capable of it, just as she knew that her mother wasn't.

Giovanni's eyes rolled as he picked up a chair and staggered towards his wife. Eventually, he managed to sit with his face about a foot from hers. She withdrew a little from his vaporous breath but otherwise continued knitting as if he wasn't there until he snatched the needles from her hands and threw them to the floor.

'Not hungry?' she asked mockingly.

'Let me tell you about heart, you cold bitch,' he slurred, his face and voice becoming melancholy. 'A heart has stopped every time you eat a pig that I've slaughtered and every time you eat a fish that Mario has gutted. It takes hearts to fill your precious stomachs.'

'My God, spare me. I hate it when you get soppy. What do I care about that? It's just nature's way to survive.'

'And what about Fabio? Was that nature's way too?'

'Why do you keep bringing that up? What's it to do with me? It was fourteen years ago. It was stupid men fighting a stupid men's war.'

'Get fucked, Luigia. You'll never understand.'

'You're a disgrace. Children! Leave now! Go!'

'Heart is duty, heart is willingness to sacrifice oneself, to pay the ultimate price for your fellow soldier, family and country.'

'Listen to yourself. You get all sentimental when you're drunk. I worry about the present while you're still stuck in the past. What do I care about the past? By the time you sense something, it's already in the past and meant to be forgotten. And all this pointless sacrifice you talk about. The way Mussolini is going, it's bound to happen all over again, and for what? What do we ever learn? What good ever comes of it? The poor either die or get poorer. Why should I care about all that when I have five children to raise?'

'Fabio…' Giovanni had to pause. Tears welled in his eyes. 'He was my best friend.'

'I know all that. Why keep going on about it?'

'You don't know all of it.'

'I don't want to know. There were millions of Fabios.'

Giovanni ignored her. He spoke to no one and he spoke to the universe. The children sensed a melancholic change and at once were frightened and curious.

'He was killed at Caporetto. Why him and not me I will never understand. I wanted to hold back on our attack but he refused.' A sob broke through his line of defence and tears fell in vain onto the table. 'He was so much braver than me. I should have died. He was the greater loss.' Again he paused, unable to continue for a moment his counter-attack against the barrage of emotion he was subjected to. 'A shell exploded in the trees above us and a piece of wood ripped his chest open. I could see his heart pumping and I watched it until it stopped.' His entire body shook and he cried uncontrollably now. 'There was nothing I could do. I sat there and watched, shells were bursting all around but I didn't care, and I held his hand until it stopped and then I wished with all my heart that I was dead too. His heart stopped, just like that, and all I could do was watch him and hold his hand and say stupid things to him that I can't remember. There was nothing else to be done.'

He'd not mentioned the gruesome details to his family before. For fourteen years he'd kept it under lock and key, but now, in a drunken delirium, it had poured forth like the inevitable detonation of so many years of suppressed grief.

'I'm sorry,' replied Luigia matter-of-factly. 'But it means nothing to me. I say again, I have my own problems.' She went on wearily, knowing and accepting the futility, but went on all the same. 'Again I say to you that you should let your dead be dead to rest in peace and think of your family for once instead of drinking yourself into stupidity. Put all those spirits of yours back into the bottle and leave them there.'

'Tell me, Luigia, where will I lay them to rest? In your warm bosom? You're a piece of frozen ground, a wasteland, nothing more, where nothing can be buried.'

'I do what I have to do to survive. You should too but you're weak. You blame the past, you blame your wife, you blame your shitty job, you blame everyone and everything but yourself,' she added, with vicious scorn, 'and then what little you earn you give to the publican, like a fool, instead of to your family as a responsible father should.'

The children watched and listened surreptitiously. They were afraid, too frightened to move in spite of Luigia's order for them to leave. There was so much they didn't understand but they sensed the ugly undertones and were fearful of where it might end. They could sense this was a bad one. Their mother seemed to be her usual self: hard as an anvil, uncompromising and unforgiving, but perhaps more weary than usual. It was their father they feared.

To Natalia at least, he seemed completely unstable, something like a volcano approaching its time. She couldn't quite capture his essence, what he wanted, what was missing. He seemed like the *jota*, with all the ingredients thrown together, simmering on the stove. He seemed incredibly sad and utterly defeated. His head swayed and his shoulders slumped, he was unsteady, and his eyes held in them a distant fog which made clear vision impossible. He seemed so frail at that moment that Natalia had to resist the urge to rush to his side and nurse him back to good health. Once or twice, a wistful smile came to his face but mostly there was pain, deep unremitting pain of the most horrid kind.

'This is all a waste of time. A painful waste… I loved you once, Luigia, remember? My little Gia. I loved you more than anything. You saved me in those hard years of the war and the ones that followed. Then we had children and you forgot about me. I didn't matter any more. Our love, our passion, flew away like doves from a rooftop.'

'For the love of God, listen to yourself! You're a fool. A hopeless, drunken, sentimentalist is what you've become.'

'I needed love, that's all, and for a while you gave it to me but then you turned into a miser for that just like for everything else.'

'Go and eat. Your brain must be hungry.' Luigia insolently retrieved her knitting from the floor and resumed her task, dismissing him in the process.

Natalia sensed a dangerous change in Giovanni. His mood darkened and surely her mother sensed it too but she seemed not to care in the least.

He stared at her threateningly, his jaw tightened and his mouth hardly seemed to move as he spoke. 'Get me my dinner.'

She refused to look at him. She would not yield. She must have known what was coming but merely continued with her knitting. Her impertinence climaxed with the slurping of the last of her coffee. The children, meanwhile, remained inert spectators, too frightened to say or do anything, with the exception of Mario, who prepared himself to leap at his father if necessary.

'I've already told you, get it yourself.'

Giovanni did not raise his voice. Rather, he spoke with an icy, murderous tone that made Mario rise from his seat and take a step forward from the shadows.

'Sit down, idiot,' he said to Mario. 'For the last time, Luigia, and before I do something we both might regret, get me my dinner.'

'And for the last time, no!'

A log flared in the stove. The kitchen seemed to shimmer and the light intensified for some moments, making the dark darker and the faces crueller. From her position tucked just behind Mario, Natalia saw her father's face, or at least the half that wasn't in shadow, and that was sufficient to sting her to action.

'Aniça,' she hissed, 'go and get the policeman. Hurry.'

'What for?'

'Go…now…quickly.'

Aniça obeyed. She took a lantern and left. Only Natalia and Giuseppe seemed to notice her rapid departure. Giuseppe began to cry, fretting that his sister had gone out alone in the dark. Natalia did her best to console him while, within the growing virulence of the room, she was also in need of consoling; but that would not be forthcoming.

Behind Giovanni's half visible face was Caporetto all over again, like a recurring boil that just kept filling with pus. To those who hadn't been there, it was just a name, tossed around like Waterloo or the Somme, where thousands of the largely forgotten had died. How could you ever explain to those who weren't there what it was like? Impossible. The least he could expect was some respect; demand it; he'd earned it by facing death every day and doing his duty. He wanted his sacrifice, and

Fabio's, to be acknowledged, forever remembered as if it all happened yesterday.

He resisted in every way he could the indifference that came with the passing of time, but he was losing the cruel battle against forgetfulness and indifference, just as he was losing the destructive battle against the bottle. Solace was to be found only at the pub, with his fellow veterans, indulging in drink, frivolous talk and cheap entertainment. Everything seemed to be a colossal failure and a gigantic nothingness. It had all been for nothing, which meant that he was nothing, and now he couldn't even get his ungrateful wife to get his dinner. It was too much. His own dignity, or what was left of it, and the dignified memory of Fabio and what he had endured and given, were at stake. Someone had to be accountable for all this tragedy. More often than not, it was the families of the war veterans that settled the account.

'Putana!' he suddenly screamed as he lunged.

He became a wild animal. Tier upon tier of inner hurt was suddenly directed outwards to this ancient foe with the indiscriminate ferocity of a siege gun. He went for Luigia's throat but his drunken attack was easily thwarted and all he succeeded in doing was falling to the floor, dragging her down with him, where they became intertwined as if in sordid foreplay. He struck Luigia on the face and was poised to strike again when Mario attacked him with a kick to the head that left him stunned. In that brief moment of time, Mario tried to drag his father off his mother but lacked the strength.

People talk about the quick or the dead but most people wouldn't know, they just talk through their arses, but Giovanni knew all right. He'd survived an ambush or two, but you have to recover from the initial shock quickly, quicker than anyone else, or you're a dead man. Giovanni swung his forearm and it found its mark, sending Mario reeling as if struck by a catapult.

Little Giuseppe could only stare in horror at something he could make no sense of. Natalia and Nina screamed in vain. The father turned his murderous attention on his son, grabbed him by the throat and pinned him against the wall. He punched his face again and again until Luigia broke the fabled wooden spoon, that had survived for millennia and faithfully served in the production of countless meals, on her husband's solid head.

Giovanni went insane. No meter has ever been devised to measure the level of his rage. Was this all there was left of his life, all that he was worthy of: an insubordinate wife, a son who would kill him as soon as look at him, his daughters' hysterical screams, the terror in the face of his youngest son?

There was a knife on the kitchen table. It was always blunt but it would do the job. Giovanni reached for it with a hand that no longer seemed to be his own. His wits had deserted him and he was now under the command of his rage. Everything was so slow, painfully slow, beyond everything and composed of elusive answers to ridiculous questions. Everything – his life, the war, his family, his work and even the friends he got drunk with – was ridiculous and they all played their part in creating a never-ending spiral that kept going down and down, deeper and deeper, like fetid water down a blocked drain.

Then he looked at the knife in this stranger's hand and it shocked him. 'OK, big shot, now what? You picked it up, what are you going to do with it? Kill your own flesh and blood? Kill your wife? Kill yourself in front of this little audience? Is this what it's all about? Is this the action of a hero?'

Like most men, he liked to be thought of as decisive. But now, he thought, if it had been him or me in an ambush, all this uncertainty and hesitation meant that he would have been dead in an instant and become merely another casualty of war, another carcass marked by a cross stuck in the earth. He wasn't a soldier any more, he was something else; something intervened. He raised the knife to save face as much as anything else, but it was all theatre now as he dramatically dropped it to the floor, enjoying the powerful clattering sound it made and hoping that the others enjoyed it too. Was it true then? Was he just mad, plain and simple? Shell-shocked like everyone else?

There was no applause at the end of his performance even though he had shown mercy and spared them all. Little did they know how close they had come to death and at that moment he would not be able to put into words what had stopped him. He had given them a small taste of what it was like when being close to death was a way of life. Perhaps they might have learned something that words alone could never teach but the look he saw in their faces gave him little satisfaction for, instead of understanding, he saw terror. He drew himself to his full height and made what he thought was a dignified exit only to find, standing in his way, a policeman who looked like he'd had enough of attending another drunken ex-serviceman's domestic.

At the hearing before the magistrate in Trieste, Natalia and Nina were required to testify. Natalia was questioned about that night and others like it. There were no questions about her father's funny side, his loving side and, at times, of his genuine kindness. In the end, the magistrate said he was sick and tired of drunks behaving in this way towards their families, war or no war, and locked him up for one to two years. (I am not sure exactly how long the sentence was.)

On his release, he did not return home. He never did.

4

Natalia's life entered a new phase, a common one in the early to mid twentieth century but still painful on a personal level, a fatherless one. She never visited him in prison; she thought about it but Luigia convinced her and the rest of them that it really wasn't a place for children and no way for a child to have to see a parent, in a zoo made for people. Natalia heeded her mother's advice. It was hard to go against her mother's harsh yet wise truths, but what could she say to him and how could she even look at him when she had been a part of the process leading to his incarceration? Yes, it was for the best and much less painful to simply stay away.

Needless to say, Giovanni's income was missed. Life suddenly became harder still. There was a lot more work to be done by all of them but, being the eldest, the lion's share fell to Mario and Natalia. Only Giuseppe, the great hope, was afforded the liberty and privilege to prolong his schooling.

Almost daily, Luigia bemoaned her husband's drunken stupidity that caused them to be in this predicament. Her opinion was that he was weak; a failure who shirked his responsibilities and lacked the fortitude required to raise a family in a hard world. He'd chosen instead to indulge himself in drunken frivolity at the local pub, with his equally flawed companions, at his family's expense, and she despised him for it.

Natalia took on some of her mother's resentment. Her father was now a common criminal, a prisoner, and because of that, their lives had become so much harder. He had betrayed his family and thus forfeited any right to be loved. There was only work, duty and sacrifice now and the family had to pull together to survive by selling food, fish and whatever else they could produce to supplement Mario's meagre earnings. Natalia learned what a cruel world it was, what a merciless world it was, a world that owed you nothing and demanded struggle to get from one day to the next. There was no joy, no affection, no fun; her father had taken all that with him and she cursed him for that too, for stealing from her the little golden snippets of childhood.

Her mother was cold and utilitarian, she had to be, and her focus was solely on getting by with no regret whatsoever for the absence of little pleasures. Pleasures were luxuries that were not affordable. Natalia rarely got the chance to play with friends and could never bring any of them home, her mother wouldn't allow it, so the moments that she had free of tasks were mainly spent reading books, sewing and creating beautiful things out of nothing with her *'mani di fata'*.

In fact, Natalia had few friends. She cherished her solitude. Small talk repelled her and she shunned superficial pleasures and people. She contented herself with her sisters, her books and her creativity. She preferred to be alone; people disappointed, they judged and most of the time they simply wanted something. Those who were better educated looked down on her, she often felt that sting, while her equals thought her aloof, snobbish and conceited, but in actual fact she was deeply insecure. At its root lay a profoundly pessimistic nature, a deep sense of caution, an intense fear of failure and the deeply disturbing thought that she didn't belong. As a consequence, she nurtured a strong and self-preserving distrust of others as well as a terrible envy of anyone she considered had reached above her, especially those of lesser merit who had merely benefitted from opportunity. She smiled infrequently and almost never laughed. Her seriousness was legendary and nothing ever came easily to her to lighten her mood. She despised those who had opportunities she never had, particularly if they were squandered, as well as those who seemed to get everything so easily, without the least sacrifice or effort. It stoked her fierce sense of the unfairness of life in general and hers in particular.

For Natalia, life as a wife and mother would never be enough. She wanted and expected more of herself. She wanted a career and independence and the security and fulfilment that went with it. Schooling having been denied her meant that she had to turn to her hands to establish a career.

5

It is hard to imagine what life in Italy in 1937 must have been like. The Spanish Civil War, pitting republican forces against fascist ones, provided a stark overture to what was to come. Maniacs ruled in Italy, Germany and the Soviet Union and the unthinkable, another world war, in such a short time since the end of the war that was supposed to end all wars, seemed increasingly inevitable.

But Natalia, now aged sixteen, had no interest in such things; for her it was a good year. She took an apprenticeship as a seamstress and began earning a little money. She kept a little for herself but most went to her mother, which had the immediate effect of improving her status within the family and the esteem in which her mother held her.

To an intelligent, driven girl, her ability to earn was a seminal event; a crucial step towards adulthood, independence and a meaningful career. Befitting her ambition was the way she threw herself at her work in wave after wave of assaults against any fortifications which stood in the way. Just doing things well, competently, adequately, was not good enough. She hungered for perfection, praise and respect. She had to be the best.

Natalia drove herself hard and expected the same of others. Those who didn't strive were lesser people. Lazy, self-indulgent hedonists who drifted, wasted opportunities, wasted their time and the time of others, failed to grasp the importance of hurling oneself constantly at tasks of substance in order to improve oneself, achieve things that mattered, perhaps even attain greatness, barely deserved to walk the Earth.

Forward momentum was all that really mattered to Natalia. Positive purposeful strides had to be taken almost every day. This was her sole source of contentment. Commitment was her fuel, achievement her nourishment, and conversely, stagnation brought despair.

But two years later, Natalia was to learn once more that life rarely proceeds entirely to plan and that, yes, it can be very unfair. The Second World War threw a spanner in her works as, in an instant, food out-ranked fine clothes, the desirable gave way to the essential, and the war effort trumped everything else. She resented the idea that stupid decisions made by stupid people altered the direction of her life and that she was powerless to stop it. It meant a halt to her creation of beautiful clothes and a return to domestic duties, vegetable growing and market stalls. The unprecedented scale of world tumult meant nothing to her other than to reinforce her opinion of humanity as fundamentally flawed and stupid, creating a world where the deserving are thwarted and the undeserving succeed.

Many, many years later, in the quiet of her nursing home room, she spoke to me softly, her voice by then enfeebled with age and sickness. She spoke with more than just her usual bitterness. It was with the bitterness acquired over a lifetime that attends the final humiliating and unconditional surrender. Natalia had always had a leaning to the left side of politics, being sympathetic to but staunchly detached from the working class, but none of that seemed to matter so much to her any more as she gave me her bleakly cynical insights on the human condition and enlarged on her deprecation of the masses. These are the pearls she left me with.

'The first in school are always the last in life,' Natalia proclaimed, in her usual tone that implied an unquestionable universal truth. She had already told me this so many times that it was there, in my subconscious, as if part of my brain had been turned into a stone tablet onto which those profound words had been chiselled. I don't know whether there is any truth to it or not, you'd have to ask all those clever sociologists, and I guess you'd also have to ask those 'fortunate' enough not to have had much of an education whether their life really is all the better for it. All I can say with any certainty is that misfortune affects all of us and I would prefer educated and unfortunate to uneducated and unfortunate every day of the week.

Her next two pronouncements were entirely new to me and came as a complete surprise. They revealed a deep cynicism about how the world operates, a profound resentment at how things had gone with her, but perhaps also a deep and incisive awareness.

'If you can talk and stop others from talking over the top of you, then you will become a great leader, even a prime minister or president.' She elaborated by saying that no other qualification was needed and it didn't matter if what you said was true or false. This naturally led to her second point: 'People will follow a bucket of shit as long as it's not seen to be leaking.'

I was stunned by this. I was still young. Was this the passing on of wisdom from a mother to her son? I can't remember exactly what I said in reply but it was something inept like did she need more fruit?

But now that I am older and wiser, as they say, with more than a few years of reflection under my belt, I can see more than a little grain of truth in what she said, but more than that, I can see more clearly what it reveals about her. She was intensely individualistic and would never mindlessly echo the talk or actions of others. She was never a sheep and would never submit to populist ideas. She quickly saw through mere demagoguery and craved and admired in its stead talk of substance, provided that it was backed up by deeds. She was also a colossal snob. She had few friends and chose them very carefully. She didn't want to hang around with what she would consider time-wasters. She was totally uncompromising about that because her time was precious and best spent on personal advancement; to fritter time away was to take a backward step and that was anathema.

For a woman with such a nature to then suffer the devastations that she went through, of one defeat after another, left her completely shattered in body and mind. All that remained to her then was the quicksand of self-pity into which she sank.

6

In mid-1940, Natalia returned to full time work at a factory in Trieste making uniforms for the armed forces. This pleased her because it was a step in the right direction. The work of course was repetitive and did not require any great skill. However, she was doing something that God had gifted her a talent for and she fully intended to make the most of the opportunity by being the best at her job in the entire factory. She achieved that feat.

Her male supervisor frequently plied her with praise while putting his arms around her waist from behind. The praise was whispered seductively into either ear and from such close range that she could feel his lips working against the lobe. Quite often, she felt something else as well, further down.

Natalia, being intensely modest, found his unwelcome advances most distasteful. She wished he wouldn't do it but dared not risk offending him for fear of losing her job. She enjoyed the praise he bestowed on her but it goes without saying she would have preferred to have it proffered on more conventional lines. The manner of its proffering also raised doubts in her mind about its validity: was the praise genuinely related to her work or was it merely intended to procure sexual favours? Still, it was just another thing that had to be endured, just like the air raids and the shortages, but the bombs mostly fell on the port and the railways and the shortages didn't impact so heavily on those with a plot of land, so they weren't as much of a problem to her as the supervisor's liberties.

The air raids were sporadic and caused excitement that was almost welcome as respite from a life of tedious routine. An occasional plane was even shot down and tiny white parachutes would sometimes emerge

Natalia (right) with work colleagues, early 1940s.

and drift away into the distance. It was easy to forget that each represented a life, albeit the life of an enemy who would, however, one day become a friend. Fortunately for Natalia, the supervisor, and the other workers, a factory making uniforms was not considered a worthy military target, carpet bombing had not yet become an Allied tactic, and so, they were allowed to go about their business unhindered and allowed the luxury of living.

Yes, things weren't so bad. Natalia had a small but regular income again, she had a large measure of independence and, though mundane, the work honed her skills in the field she desired to pursue. Another of the advantages was that she and most of the other mainly female factory workers lived on the first floor above the factory, where they each had a small bedroom. The sole irritation was the men who visited at all hours and, with sound largely free to travel, the grotesque noises that went with their visits.

In time, Natalia's supervisor became one of the visitors. In the end, it was a pragmatic decision to submit. She was a young woman of nineteen. She wasn't living in Contovello any more. Mario wasn't there to protect her. The more she resisted, the more he advanced. Her slaps he merely seemed to find erotic. It disgusted her. He was old enough to be her father. But it was inevitable. It was the way of the world. She wanted to keep her job and that's all there was to it.

Eventually, the cursed war did have a devastating impact on Natalia. It tore her family apart. Mario joined the Italian army and wasn't heard of for years. It seemed in all likelihood that he was dead. As months and years went by, the certainty of his death tore Natalia's fragile cocoon to shreds. The loss crushed her and the waste enraged her. In quiet moments, she cried and mourned like she never had before.

At this time, Nina and Aniça were still living in Contovello and they began to hang around with some of the young boys there. Aniça befriended a dashing young chap called Marcello, nicknamed Cello, and the two sisters found themselves spending more and more time with Cello and his friends. They talked, laughed, drank, smoked, flirted and danced and threw caution to the wind with the typical delusion of invincibility that goes with youth.

As time went by, Aniça found herself falling in love with Cello and missing him more and more during those times that he would inexplicably disappear. She put his periods of absence down to his restless nature and knew that he would return to her sooner or later. However, its regular occurrence was becoming a source of frustration to her. When he did return days or weeks later, she found his moods to be unpredictable and it typically took many days for him to settle back into being the cheerful larrikin that she was so fond of. But it was becoming increasingly apparent that with each revenant there was less and less of Cello's old self and more and more of a stranger who was on edge, distracted and concerned. Aniça feared infidelity but dared not raise that spectre. His freedom of spirit was one of the things that she loved about him and she feared that any attempt on her part to restrict that freedom would simply drive him away, so she kept quiet, accepted things as they were, and hoped that in time he would grasp her love and love her as much as she loved him.

Then for a long time Cello did not return and Aniça despaired. There was no news of him at all, so she had no idea where he was or what he was doing or who for that matter he might be with. He had inexplicably disappeared without a trace, leaving her mind a fertile plot for all manner of imaginings, chief of which was his death or his philandering.

The mystery was solved on the day that the SS came to arrest Nina and Aniça for their association with members of the *partigiani* (partisans). Nina, Aniça and Cello and some of his colleagues spent the remainder of the war in German labour camps. Their experiences can only be imagined as they were never spoken of but somehow all three of them managed to survive the war and, what's more, Aniça would go on to marry Cello and fuss over him till the day he died.

7

Guido Kakovich was born on 21 November 1919. He grew up in the coastal town of Piran, on the Istrian peninsula, in what is now Slovenia. At the time, Pirano, as it was known under Italian rule, was a small fishing village, and not much more than a stone's throw from Trieste.

He was the youngest of nine children born to Giovanni and Antonia Kakovich, four boys and five girls. We have no photos of Giovanni but there is one of Antonia which reveals an attractive woman with a serious disposition and lovely eyes.

Guido completed elementary school then left to take up a trade as a barber. He was thirteen when his father died and sixteen when his mother died, which left him nominally under the care of his older brother Guerrino. For reasons that are not entirely clear, Guido never developed any strong or lasting bonds with any of his siblings. It seems that from a young age he was pretty much left to his own devices.

At the outbreak of war, Guido joined the Italian navy and served on the cruiser *Duca D'Aosta*. I don't know why he joined – whether from a sense of duty, adventure, romance or money – but his heart wasn't in the fighting side of it at all. He didn't want to kill anyone and he didn't want anyone to kill him. During the war, he saw death happen right next to him, just like that, in a split second, instantly transforming a comrade into a lump of meat. It was ugly and it was wasteful. He preferred the social side, having drinks and laughs with fellow sailors and chatting with everyone on board as he cut their hair.

His heart wasn't in the business of killing but was instead back in Trieste, with a girl he'd met at a party when he was last on leave. Her name was Natalia, her family called her Dali, but he decided to call her Lina. It was softer and to him seemed to suit her better and she didn't

Guido in naval uniform, 1940.

seem to mind. She was just about all he thought about and so the men complained when, as he daydreamed away, he cut too close and nicked their skin.

Both in and out of uniform, Guido had a dashing appearance. He possessed all the vanity and assuredness of youth and had a ready, mischievous smile to go with it. His dark brown hair of regulation length was kept slicked back, he was clean-shaven, his nose was well proportioned and his deep-set eyes revealed a man of warmth, integrity and peace.

The story goes that he was immediately attracted to Natalia because of her eyes and her bottom. Their exact order remains a mystery; I have my own opinion on that which I won't divulge as it is pure conjecture. No doubt it was lust at first sight, fully in accord with the rich, perennial tradition of the drunken sailor on leave, notoriously prepared to be lib-

Natalia, circa 1943, around the time she met Guido.

eral with both money and semen; but some allowance must be made for the distortions caused by war. Everything changes 'because of the war': time, events, behaviour, rules. Everything is compressed, as if being forced into a smaller amount of space and time, because tomorrow you may be dead.

Natalia didn't like parties. She didn't consider herself to be a 'party girl'. She preferred restraint, quiet intelligent conversation with like-minded people and to be doing productive things. She found parties vulgar events where people smoked and drank too much, talked rubbish, told crude jokes, misbehaved, fell over, passed out, took inappropriate liberties and descended to all sorts of immoral conduct. Even so-called intelligent people could become utterly stupid, leaving dignity and decorum outside the door along with the muddy shoes and wet raincoats. Her protests were howled down, however, when the other young women of the factory who, like Natalia, resided on the floor above, decided that a party would be fun and promptly sent out invitations to what seemed to Natalia to be half the eligible population of Trieste.

Guido and his fellow sailors happened to be on the prowl. Somewhat slovenly now, their whites were no longer quite as white, their grooming had become dishevelled and their sensibly affordable aftershave had dissipated and been supplanted by the familiar smells of the *osteria*. They rolled along the streets of Trieste laughing at things that normally would not be funny at all. Naturally, now that the *osteria* had closed, they were looking for somewhere to kick on and have some more fun. The following week, they would be back on ship and, if the dice rolled against them, they could all end up dead. Somehow, they had to pack a lifetime of living into three days, just in case, and they were determined to do so.

They'd caught wind of a party going on at a factory somewhere and put their faith in their collective ability to sniff these things out to find it and, sure enough, they did. The hard part having been accomplished, everything else would now fall easily into place once the tipsy women saw these dashing, handsome and heroic men in their mildly tarnished uniforms.

The party was already in full swing when the sailors entered. It was everything a good party should be: loud music, dancing, laughter and the thick, warm smog of booze, boozy breath and cigarette smoke, all charged with a bit of sexual electricity. The sailors found themselves at home and made themselves at home, ripped into the cheap wine they'd brought, and yelled to be heard, whether anyone listened or not.

Guido was onto his second glass of wine, making his way slowly around the large crowded room. He chatted to a group of people who knew La Spezia very well as they had grown up there. La Spezia is a port city and naval base on the north-west coast of Italy where Guido's ship was based. They were banging on in ribald tones about its renowned red-light district that Guido was already well aware of but cared little for, when he spotted an exquisite pair of eyes not more than a few metres from him. They were not on him but they belonged to an angel who was sitting quietly on a simple chair, instead of a throne, in an act of sublime condescension. Those eyes, large, dark and perceptive, should have been adorned with all the jewels of the world, yet all they had to proclaim them was the mildest trace of make-up. She looked small, pale, fragile and very, very, serious. Thick, black, curled hair reached her shoulders and was swept away from her forehead to reveal her face in its entirety, which was round and full. Her skin looked smooth and flawless. Her mouth was small and so tight-lipped that she seemed incapable of smiling, which gave her the overall impression of sternness and distaste for what was going on. Guido drew the correct conclusion that she would be no easy nut to crack but crack her he would.

Natalia cradled a glass of wine in her lap which had barely been touched. She sat next to another young woman who, under normal circumstances, would have been most desirable indeed, yet now she existed, to her great misfortune, entirely in Natalia's shadow. They were not speaking but Guido imagined that this angel would have many wondrous things to say, but the sweet delicacy of her voice could never rise above the noise of the party, and the rabble that went with it, to make itself heard. Their eyes met for a moment before she quickly looked away, but that moment was enough; it could have been a lifetime, it could have been a millisecond, but it was enough. She was the one. She was for him. He wanted to save and protect her. He wanted to bring joy to her seriousness. He wanted to know everything about her. He wanted to be her hero and, he thought, the task of keeping her safe would at last give this shitty war some meaning.

Guido was not skilled in the art of approaching strange women with a serious demeanour; nevertheless, following the twang of Cupid's bow, he felt compelled to act and found himself floating towards her in a sozzled and dreamlike state. Before he knew it, he was speaking to her, but it was as if someone else was doing all the talking on his behalf, and that someone went by the name of alcohol.

'My name's Guido,' the alcohol said.

He offered his hand. The angel looked at it, hesitated, weighed up the situation, took it fleetingly, out of politeness more than anything else, then quickly withdrew her hand so as not to give him any cause to think that the encounter was destined to proceed any further. Her brief glance was meant to convey the same message. She looked uncomfortable, he liked that, and she was well-dressed and well-mannered, he liked that as well. She made a point of not looking at him again, of ignoring him, and he was encouraged by that because, to his way of thinking, it implied that he had struck a chord of sorts, perhaps ever so slightly, and that, as a result, she felt the need to reinforce the construct separating them. He was sure he had got under her skin in some way, even just a little; it was all there in the brief look she had given him when their hands clasped and also in the way she stiffened her spine and sat more correctly as she turned away. He felt sure that she wanted to impress him with her decorum and her aloof, hard-to-get, demeanour.

So Guido decided to test his theory. He decided to mess around with her a bit, play with her, annoy her, maybe even get her a little angry to see what she was made of, and then, reel her in slowly. It was a gamble he was by no means sure would pay off and not one he would have attempted when sober, but he had a feeling in his gut and he was willing to make the effort for this one. He didn't say another word but he didn't go away either; he simply stood and stared at her like an Easter Island statue for as long as it would take to drive her crazy. Of course, Natalia refused to acknowledge him. It was the woman sitting next to her who needlessly drew her attention to Guido's continued presence by elbowing Natalia and gesticulating toward him. She ignored her too, took a hesitant sip of her wine, and pretended to be entirely focused on the music. Guido immediately saw that his angel was stubborn and strong-willed, he liked that too, and still he stared and refused to move or to say a word. Eventually, this wore her down, it had to, for he would have done it all night to be victorious. She was worth it.

'What do you want?' Natalia hissed.

'I want to marry you,' he joked.

Natalia actually smiled and his victory was assured. 'Go away, you're an idiot.'

'Yes, I am an idiot, but are you saying that only an idiot would want to marry you?'

'I'm saying that you stand there and stare like an idiot. Go away.'

'I won't go away until we've danced.'

'No! I don't even know you and I don't dance with idiots.'

'You'll like me even more when you get to know me.'

This annoyed her, he could tell. It was, of course, meant to. Guido enjoyed annoying people.

'Who says I like you? I don't like you at all. You're rude and insolent, the way you stand there and stare. I detest rudeness.'

'It's rude not to dance with a sailor when he asks you, especially when you're already secretly in love with him.'

'I don't love you! I hate you! Now go away and leave me alone.'

This joust was all he could have hoped for and the time had come, he judged, for the next step. Before she had time to regain her composure, Guido reached over, took her glass of wine, drank it, then gave the empty glass back to her.

'You really are a horrible man. How dare you?'

He'd made an impression with his daring, her eyes told him so, and he also knew it by how flustered she had become as she sought a place to rest her empty glass. Her irritation was feigned. Her sour expression wouldn't fool an idiot. He was on firm ground now and his growing confidence made him act even more brazenly. He'd crack her little shell of respectability if it was the last thing he ever did, and with the way this crazy war was going, it very well could be.

Before she knew what hit her, Guido swooped down and kissed her on the lips, picked her up from the chair, surreptitiously had a little feel of her curvy bottom in the process, and carried her off to the dance floor. Natalia made an attempt to struggle and hissed curses and threw daggers at him with her eyes, but she hated creating a scene and the fact was that she had been a little smitten by this insane sailor, so she did not raise her voice. Guido took the greatest delight in seeing Natalia's immense embarrassment. He laughed. He was having the time of his life, dancing with his angel and returning the joyous smiles of those that were watching them.

'You're a madman!' Natalia cried, at a volume indicative of her having dispensed with another layer of decorum.

His response was to hold her tighter so that there was no gap between them now at all and no chance of her escape; and to dance harder.

'I don't like this music,' she protested.

'Too bad. I do. Now shut up and dance.'

It was an extraordinary party. Unthinkable things happened, surely none more so than when a drunken Natalia fell against a vat of wine, knocking it over and spilling wine everywhere in the process. This incident became the stuff of family legend and an unforgettable source of shame to Natalia and delight to Guido.

Guido was convinced he'd found the woman he wanted to spend the rest of his life with. Natalia, ever cautious, wasn't so sure. They were completely different in so many ways, surely incompatible, but she found that she kept thinking about him, she couldn't help it, and his antics would pop up in her mind at the oddest moments and make her smile. This annoyed and worried her because she had no control over it and she wanted to be in control, always. It also indicated to her that he'd had an effect on her and that, in spite of her reticence about such things, she had to admit to liking him, and that he gave her some pleasure. What she didn't like was the idea that she would somehow become dependent on him but she hoped that he would survive the war and that she would see him again at a future time. Natalia surprised herself by how genuine and heartfelt that feeling of hope was.

8

Whenever Guido set his mind to something, it would be easier to drag a pyramid around the world with a team of donkeys than to sway him. Since the party, his sole care was to survive this deluded, grandiose war so as to be reunited with his sweetheart Lina, who was already the only person he could think of, and the only thing in his life right now that meant anything good. They had exchanged some letters. His were passionate, hers more discreet and non-committal, but nevertheless he felt sure that she wanted to be with him after all this war nonsense was over. They simply had to survive.

He went over all the details of that night at the party, over and over again. It delighted him. It could not have gone better. It shone a light on the darkest moments and gave him hope. It helped to keep him sane and it gave him the will to go on, especially when the war turned on its head and he suddenly found himself a prisoner of the Germans, along with most of the Italian navy, being marched under guard to the railway yards of La Spezia to board a train to God only knew where and to God only knew what fate. He wanted to see Natalia again no matter what it took. He didn't want to die in some stinking, God-forsaken POW camp, worked to death for the Fuhrer. He wasn't going to die, he would find a way not to die, he would marry Natalia and they would have a family. He would find a way.

Guido had been told many times that he could talk his way in to or out of anything. He had a gift for disarming people with his charm and unpretentious candour. This maxim was to be put to the test now that he was a POW and the stakes could hardly be higher.

As the solemn line of prisoners was being marched to the railhead, Guido put his mind to work and slowly and methodically worked his way towards the back of the long line. The guard closest to him had a machine gun but he was not SS, he was middle-aged, not in the peak of fitness, and his face seemed gentler than your average German soldier.

Guido sensed hope. If he could somehow create a bond and persuade the guard of their common humanity, he might stand a chance. He decided to play the oldest card there is whenever and wherever young men get together, the same card played by Adam when he finally had a male companion with whom to talk away from Eve.

'You should see the arse on the girl I've got waiting for me back home,' he remarked casually, as though they were sitting at the bar of an *osteria* striking up conversation over a glass or two of wine instead of tramping at the end of a ragged line of miserable men where his companion held a machine gun.

'Shut up, dickhead. Don't get your hopes up. You won't be seeing her again where you're going,' replied the guard.

Despite the ominous nature of the reply, there was an absence of ferocity in his voice which implied a chink that could be worked on. Added to that was Guido's reading of the guard's demeanour, which he felt sure was that of a weary middle-aged man, probably with a family back home, who was as sick of the whole business as anyone else. Guido gauged the moment and decided to wait and see if the guard made the next move. Eventually he did, and from there it was plain sailing for the smooth-talking Guido all the way to the finish line.

'Nice arse, is it?'

'Oh, you would not believe it. My God!' Guido gestured with two cupped hands to indicate the outline of this most wondrous part of female anatomy that just might end up saving his life. 'Curvy like two melons side by side,' Guido continued. 'Every day I thank God for the eyes he gave me to see it with.'

The guard was still on edge, making sure no other guards were within earshot, but a smile of sorts had made its appearance that made his face look almost kind. 'What about her tits?'

'Oh, *Madonna mia*, the same. Soft, pale like porcelain, a good handful and some to spare.'

'My God. Where is this piece?'

'Trieste.'

'Trieste! I know Trieste. I'm Austrian. My village was about halfway between Trieste and Vienna. I've been to Trieste many times for a holiday or on my way to Venice. Nice city. Are you married to her?'

'Not yet, but I will be, and we'll have lots of kids and be very happy together.'

'Yeah, maybe, if you survive. Good luck.'

'I'll survive.'

'They all say that.'

'Yes, but I mean it. I'm lucky like that.'

'If you say so.'

They stopped talking for a bit but Guido knew that he had to maintain what momentum he had going. He felt sure that the guard's heart wasn't in all this war rubbish any more than his own and that he would sooner be safely at home with his family.

'Have you got family?' Guido asked.

'Sure, a wife and five kids.'

'Five kids! That's great. That's just what I want.'

'Good luck to you.'

'Is your wife pretty?'

'She's had five kids. What can I say, she's OK, you know, she's older now and put a bit of weight on. Nothing like your girlfriend, I bet, but she's had five kids. It takes a toll on them. But that doesn't matter. I'd be with her in a flash if I could.'

'Your kids good?'

'Very good, all of them. They've been brought up right. My eldest son has just joined the Wehrmacht.'

'You sound unhappy about that.'

'Of course I'm unhappy. He's somewhere in Ukraine. It's a death sentence. I'm Austrian. I don't give a shit about this stupid war. I just want it to be over.'

'Amen. You must miss them.'

'What do you think? Every day it's all I think about.'

'You'll see them again when all this crap is over.'

'I don't know. I've got a bad feeling. I don't think I'll come out of all this shit in one piece.'

'Don't say that. You will, I know it.'

'Bullshit. No one knows. No one knows anything.'

'You're right, we don't know anything. We're the bunnies that just do what we're told. All we can do is keep our mouths shut and keep our thoughts to ourselves while we do all the dirty work. You can't let out the feelings you have in your heart and guts.'

The guard sighed. 'Well said. You've got your head screwed on right. Better than most your age. But what's in our hearts and guts these days are bullets and shrapnel.'

Guido sensed that he had formed a workable connection with the guard. He waited, barely able to breath, for the decisive opening. He had to be patient; to act prematurely or with too much eagerness could seriously undermine the gains made so far. The timing had to be precise and correctly choosing the exact moment when the guard was most vulnerable was critical. There was no middle ground, no room for compromise; it was all or nothing. Everything hanged on it.

'You'd love to see that girl of yours with the curves again, I bet?'

Guido made a sign of the cross in case the guard was pious. 'Jesu Cristo! My God! More than anything!'

The guard paused. Guido had the sense that everything was now in the balance between the guard's morality and his duty. Had Guido made a strong enough case to convince the guard that he was a fellow human being with the same desires, an individual worthy of clemency and not just a faceless, nameless and story-less member of a miserable and defeated flock undeserving of pity.

'All right, shut up and listen,' said the guard, his eyes darting nervously in all directions. 'When I give the signal, you run, run like hell, do you understand? Keep running until you're back in Trieste, in her arms, do you hear me? Do not stop for anything or you're fucked.'

'Yes. Of course. Thank you. Thank you, my brother.'

'OK. Give her a kiss on the arse from me when you see her.'

'Don't you worry about that. I'll give her ten on each cheek from you.'

He smiled ruefully. 'I'm Albert.'

'Guido.'

'I'll never see my children again, Guido, but I hope you get some of your own. Good luck, you'll need it.'

'And you. What can I say other than thank you? I pray that your family is safe and you will see them all again.'

They approached an area where the road curved and the sides were thick with bushes. The guard looked around, all was clear, he signalled to Guido to bolt and he did, running faster than he had ever run before. The guard made as if to shoot him but Guido never looked back and in an instant he had disappeared into the bushes.

Guido walked, ran and hitched rides all the way back to Trieste. He didn't stop until he was reunited with his beloved Lina.

9

Guido and Natalia were married in the cathedral of San Giusto in Trieste on the first day of October 1944. Normally on such occasions, people pray for good weather, but on this day they prayed for the non-occurrence of air raids instead, and on this occasion their prayers were favourably answered.

Unfortunately, no photos have survived of this event. Over time, they have been lost or deliberately destroyed. More's the pity. Still, as often as not, a marriage is not worth the paper it is written on and the most solemn vows, spoken in such sacred tones, tend to disappear, gradually like vapours on the wind or tempestuously like ice in a furnace.

The newly weds moved into a rented house in Servola, a comfortable middle-class suburb in the leafy hills to the east of central Trieste. The rent was very reasonable for such an area where they found themselves nestled amongst teachers, professors, nurses and such. The view from the house took in the local church, San Lorenzo, and in the distance, the Adriatic.

The property had a high stone fence, sturdy iron gates and a pretty garden, with lots of roses amongst which chickens scratched around. There was even a pond, but it was always dry. Perhaps it leaked. The house was made of the same stone and was multilevel with a cellar, ground floor and upper floor. It was comfortable enough, more than enough, and while Guido did any sort of work he could get his hands on, Natalia relished her new role of making the home and garden perfect.

Natalia was not and never had been physically strong. She did the lighter tasks and naturally directed Guido on how to do the heavier tasks to her own satisfaction. He quite enjoyed her bossiness and exaggerated scolding. To him, it proved that she loved him and also led to the bestowing upon him of much sympathy from male friends and colleagues who weren't married. He went along with performing the role of subject and supplicant with his usual humour and wit. He loved it all: his wife, making a home and working hard to make it all happen. There was direction now, a compass course towards the goal of having children. All that remained was for the war to go away.

Good food was prepared every day. They had their own fresh eggs, fruit and vegetables. In his spare time, Guido went fishing and almost always brought home a fish or two. Natalia kept the house tidy and spotless, she made new curtains and beautiful clothes for them. The garden was cared for and thrived. Everything they could have hoped for was coming true and then, when the war did finally end and everyone had somehow survived – Mario, Nina, Aniça and Cello – it was like a miracle had happened and they were truly blessed.

After the war, Guido joined the police force. With that came the prospect of steady work with reasonable pay and the opportunity of advancement for effort.

In that light, thoughts naturally turned to having children and raising them in a perfect family home in a desirable neighbourhood complete with good schools and other amenities. But some disquiet lurked. There existed an unspoken source of anxiety with possible ramifications. As the saying goes, the white tablecloth always has a hidden stain.

At some time in 1944, I don't know exactly when but likely to be in the lead-up to their wedding, Natalia had an abortion. Guido wanted to keep the baby but Natalia decided against it. I can only suppose that her decision was made 'because of the war' and because they were unmarried. We know that Guido wanted to keep the baby, and one reason was the war, so that if he died tomorrow at least a child of his would live on. Guido was very upset by her decision. He tried to change her mind but couldn't. The pain of that loss stayed with him but he never spoke about it with me and only very rarely with Adi.

It was a backyard job somewhere in Trieste. In a Catholic country in 1944, it had to be very backyard indeed – the furthest back of the deepest yard. There are no details of course but it was successfully kept quiet at the time. Other than that, all we know is that it was a boy and that there was some infection afterwards, apparently mild, but nevertheless with potential consequences for Natalia's future fertility.

But fears of the possibility of infertility were eventually dispelled when husband and wife became father and mother on the thirtieth day of June 1946. It was a girl, Adriana, forever to be known as Adi, and as happens whenever a child is born, it was a life-changing event, more for the mother than the father, as, particularly back in 1946, was generally the case.

Guido was now a police officer in the Venezia-Giulia region. For him, life simply went on pretty much as before, except that now at the end of the working day he had a baby daughter to love and fuss over, in delightful snippets of time.

For Natalia of course the change was immense and, I'm quite sure, not entirely to her liking. She'd come to almost hope that she couldn't fall pregnant and now that she was a mother, it spelled the end of her career as a seamstress and any prospect of independence. It was another blow to which the other cheek must be turned, the same cheek that was turned when she was pulled from school at a young age to support her family.

At the time, it was all put down to sleep deprivation, fatigue, a nervous disposition and difficulty with adjustment; all this restlessness and discontent and complete anhedonia. It wasn't called post-natal depression, not back then; after all, what could she possibly be depressed about? She had a good man with a good job and money coming in, if not in abundance, then at least regularly and with the comforting prospect of more to come in the future. Each month, Guido brought his pay packet home intact, took a little for himself and left the rest for Natalia to use as she saw fit. He trusted her in that way because he knew that she would not be wasteful with it. Also, she had her extended family nearby and she could count on their support, the home and garden were to be envied and she had a beautiful, healthy daughter. Depression was out of the question as there was absolutely no rational cause for it.

But having a child is a major adjustment. The previous life is forsaken and a new life of duty and responsibility is commenced. Being maternal and nurturing did not come naturally to Natalia. In fact, it barely came at all. She seemed to struggle with most aspects of motherhood. Her breasts were unproductive, so Adi was raised on goat's milk. That important bond was lost. Fundamentally, Natalia lacked the characteristics of selflessness and want of personal ambition that goes with being a good mother; rather, she was fundamentally selfish as well as harbouring narcissistic tendencies, which had the effect of relegating motherhood to a state of intrusion that must be endured.

Gradually, telltale chinks appeared. The house became untidy and wasn't cleaned for weeks. The garden was less attended to. Dead flower heads appeared on the roses. Natalia looked tired and unhappy. Pleasure had drifted from their lives. There were the first signs of tension in the marriage as Guido wanted to live life as before but Natalia found that impossible. He couldn't understand why she was so unhappy. Had he done something wrong? Nothing he did cheered her. Surely she had everything a woman could possibly desire but it wasn't enough; to him, it seemed that nothing was ever enough.

Gradually, Natalia's misery and ingratitude began to irritate Guido to the extent that he began to withdraw from her. Like most people at that time, he was unaware of depression as an actual illness. Its causes and its effect were a mystery. Sure, people got depressed when someone died, but otherwise it just seemed to be a cop-out for people who simply couldn't cope with the ups and downs of life. But for Natalia the depression was real, although I believe she would not have called it such. Put simplistically, life how she knew it and how she'd planned it was gone and she saw no way of getting it back.

Around this time, Natalia's trademark pessimism worsened to the extent that she began to exhibit a cruel edge to her nature. Adi recalls that when she was three years old she was unwell with whooping cough, so as a comfort she slept between her parents during this time. Her constant coughing was very distressing and kept her parents awake for much of the night. Guido remained calm and patient with her and consoled her, but Natalia would become irritable and scold her; she even elbowed and pinched her daughter in a vain attempt to get her to stop coughing as if it is within a child's control to stop coughing when suffering with pertussis. Adi has never forgotten this sign of her mother's meanness and, unfortunately, it was a foretaste of things to come.

In the end, Guido had to move Adi, placing himself between mother and daughter to stop his daughter being hurt. Finally, Natalia decided to sleep in another room until her daughter was well again. So began an unbreakable bond and a fathomless love between father and daughter. He was to be her shield and shelter for the rest of his life, repaid by the deepest love and devotion imaginable.

Natalia, circa 1949.

10

By 1950, the marriage was well and truly teetering. A creeping fog had enveloped the lives of husband and wife that left them floundering and directionless. Were men and women even designed to live together long term without driving each other crazy? By this time, Guido would say not. He did everything he could to make his darling Lina happy but he was invariably left to scratch his head. He worked hard, helped as much as he could, worked to exhaustion to make the house and garden to her liking, tried to be romantic, tried to make her laugh, tried desperately to get back some of what they'd had; but it became very clear that what they'd had for such a short time was gone.

Affection was gone. Hugs were gone. Sex had withered. Guido had to beg. I know nothing about my parents' sex life. It certainly wasn't talked about. I found my father's porn magazines one time – that cost me a kick up the backside – but it is hard for me to conceive of my mother as a sexual being. Constant rejection and always being physically pushed away took its toll on him. The humiliation he endured inevitably turned to resentment, which made him try less and less to please her and focus instead more on what he enjoyed, with or without her. He spent less time with his wife and more time with his daughter, his friends, or alone: fishing, gardening, tending his fruit and vegetables or tinkering in the shed.

Natalia couldn't understand why this was so when she was doing everything possible to raise their daughter in the right way. He didn't seem to understand that it took every ounce of her energy, and his thoughtlessness made her angry. Little things about the other began to annoy them and both felt keenly the unfairness and disappointment and loss of empathy that seemed to go with married life.

Natalia, Guido and Adriana at left, with two female cousins of Guido and their families, circa 1953.

It gnawed at Guido constantly, how everything seemed to be going wrong despite his best efforts. He criticised her negativity, she berated his silly positivity. Common ground and kindness seemed to be forever shrinking, extracted bit by bit until all that was left was a bitter pile of tailings.

In 1953, Natalia met a man to her liking. We don't know his name; we don't know much about him at all other than the fact that he was a cellist in a local orchestra. He was serious, refined, and a reader of literature and poetry. He maintained his dignity, as Natalia would have observed, by not clowning around all the time. His circle of friends was like-minded; not the eclectic, boorish, riff-raff preferred by Guido. Natalia and the cellist could have quiet meaningful conversations together over dinner or a casual glass of wine without all the foolishness, crassness and childish pranks she had to suffer at the hands of Guido in the name of fun. The cellist revitalised her while also filling her with wistful regrets about the choices she had made thus far, and this in turn created an urge within her to abandon marriage, motherhood and to start a new life with him. He was the one she should have married.

So began an affair that raised her spirits. Her weariness lifted when she saw him and each time it became harder to part and return to a life of drudgery. He did not belittle her lack of education; rather, he respected her underlying intelligence, and she preferred nothing better than to sit, quietly sipping wine and listen to him play his magnificent instrument.

I don't know how it started, how long it went on for or how Guido found out. Perhaps he sensed the change in Natalia's mood and became suspicious. It would have been difficult to keep an affair with a performing cellist secret for long. Guido never spoke about it to me and he spoke only superficially about it to Adi but what is clear is that one evening the inevitable confrontation occurred.

'I'm going out,' said Natalia in a crisp, defiant tone.

She was going out a lot more now and always announced it with a somewhat awkward and defensive edge in her voice.

'Where?' replied Guido.

'To listen to some music.'

'We can all go then.'

'It's classical, you wouldn't like it.'

'I like some classical. I'm willing to try.'

'There's no dancing, laughing or drinking and Adi would get restless. You can't have kids, and adults for that matter, mucking around when there's classical music.'

'You don't want us there, do you?'

'It's not that, it just wouldn't be your thing.'

'You've changed, Lina. You go out a lot more, by yourself.'

'Oh, you wouldn't want me to do any socialising, would you? Heaven forbid. It's OK for you, though, isn't it?'

'OK, go, but after you've seen him, don't bother coming back.'

Natalia knew that this moment would come but it still shocked her. He knows!

'Seen who? What are you talking about?'

'You're not a good liar, do you know that?'

'How dare you! Lying about what? I'm not lying!'

'The cellist, that's what you're lying about.'

Natalia took some time to recover herself. For a moment, she couldn't speak and her silence effectively established her guilt. She was unprepared, as she had not given any thought on how to react when her husband found out. The cellist was not famous but he was quite well known in Trieste and some acquaintances of Natalia had seen them together on several occasions; friends of Guido had probably seen them together too, so it was just a matter of time before it all came out.

Having collected her wits, she determined on a course of defiance and assertion. 'I'm leaving you, Guido, for good.'

Guido, though stunned, was never one to debase himself by begging or grovelling; his pride was too strong for that. If she didn't want him, she didn't want him; so be it.

He spoke slowly and deliberately, with ice in his voice. 'OK, go, I won't stop you, but Adi stays here with me.'

'Fine.' Natalia turned to go and Guido made no attempt to stop her. 'I'll come back for my things later.'

'You'll find them out on the street.'

'If that's how it's to be.'

'Yes, that's how it's to be.'

She couldn't wait to get away, to escape from this man and this life, to be with the one that she was made to be with.

She turned to her daughter, who was crying, and bent down to her. She held her shoulders and spoke softly to Adi. 'Mamma has to go away, Adi.'

'No, Mamma, don't go, I don't want you to.'

'Adi, listen to me, you have to be brave now. I will visit you.'

Adi broke free of her mother's grip, lunged at her and hugged her tightly. Natalia had no time for this sentimentality; she simply wanted to make her exit as quickly and as painlessly as possible to leave all this foolishness behind and be with the person she loved. If only she had not been so stupidly impulsive back then. She wasn't normally impulsive, she took pride in that fact, but on that occasion she had been and had paid a heavy price for it. Ah, how much better her life could have been.

She tried to tear herself away from her daughter but Adi simply refused to let go. Adi cried and begged and screamed and clung to her mother with all her strength so that she was dragged along the floor as Natalia made for the door. But Natalia never reached the door. She relented, her will conquered by her daughter's fierce tenacity, love and refusal to allow the family to disintegrate.

In the wake of such drama, there could only be an uneasy truce. Not one of them ever forgot that moment, nor entirely forgave. A part of the family fabric was torn beyond repair, patched certainly, but never to be the same again.

11

Natalia never forgot a slight upon her, or a debt incurred. She was neither forgiving nor magnanimous. You would expect, rather than being forced to rack up a loan with a loan shark's interest rate, a daughter's debt to her mother to be written off as a matter of course, put down to a mother's duty, perhaps to be redeemed in the future by a daughter's devotion when her mother became ill or old. Natalia's deep bitterness, the result of so many wounds and regrets, but also simply a part of her temperament, meant that this was never going to be the case between her and her daughter.

I go back now a few years. It was a warm, sunny July day. Adi, four years old, was just home from kinder. The coffee was cooking on the stove and filled the house with its wondrous aroma. Also on the stove, but set aside, was a pot of hot minestrone. She served herself a bowl and a piece of bread. She liked her soup piping hot, still does, and blew on each spoonful but still burned her mouth several times. She was an impatient eater, so the hungrier she was, the more her mouth was scalded.

The colours from the charming garden seemed to pour in through each window; each, surely, as good as, if not better than, a Monet. Between spoonsful, she looked at her mother with envy. She admired her elegant ways, her dress, her hair, the capable way she did things, her effortless creativity. It seemed to her that her mother could do anything she set her mind to and do it well; anything except kindness. Adi hoped that she could go out and play with the other kids in the street after lunch but she dared not mention it because her mother would almost certainly refuse, so she hoped to slip out quietly without being noticed, ignore her mother's angry calls, and worry about the consequences when she returned.

Adi was already wary of her mother, of her dark moods and intangible inconsistencies. Just like her father, she discovered that she could never please her no matter what she did or how hard she tried. She was discovering also that her mother could be vengeful and cruel and that she seemed to take a perverse delight in being so. Her mother did not seem to want to be liked, by her or anyone else; what she wanted was respect.

Everything was better when Adi's father was around – there was fun, laughter and warmth. But he seemed to be around less these days. He was always working, coming home at all hours because of his shift-work, and now he was also studying to become a customs officer. More and more, it was just her and her domineering mother, with all the discomfort that went with that. Sometimes there was joy, sometimes they laughed together, but not often.

Today was different. Natalia made herself a cup of coffee and beckoned Adi to sit with her. She took dignified sips from time to time from the fine china cup as she removed money from an ornate jewellery box she'd received as a wedding present. She counted the money and arranged it into neat piles. The box had a lock and its gold-plated key rested on the table next to the orderly piles of money. Money was important to Natalia and treated almost with reverence, for it meant security.

'Look at this money very carefully, Adi, because I was going to use it to buy myself a mink coat.'

Adi didn't know if she was meant to respond in some way. She kept sipping her soup.

Her mother stopped counting and looked up at her. She seemed annoyed. 'Did you hear what I said?'

Adi quickly swallowed her soup. It was still too hot and she grimaced as she felt it burn her gullet.

'Yes, Mamma.'

'What's wrong, Adi? Did you not understand what I said?'

'No, I mean yes, the soup was hot that's all.'

'I talked to your kinder teacher today, Adi. She said some very nice things about you that made me feel proud. She told me you are very bright and have a gift for music, so this is my gift for your gift. Instead of a mink coat for myself, I'm going to buy a piano, for you, and you will begin having lessons with a teacher right here in Servola, tomorrow.'

Adi squealed, jumped up and, before she knew what she was doing, gave her mother an unseemly squeeze. Her mother's response was warm but controlled and brief. In a moment, she held her daughter at arm's length to speak with her seriously.

'Now calm down and listen to me, Adriana. You are not standard, do you understand? You are special. I give you this gift but with it come responsibilities. Are you listening to me?'

'Yes, Mamma.'

'I make this sacrifice for you but in return I expect you to work hard, I expect you to excel. I will not tolerate laziness or poor results. I'm not giving up my mink coat to give you this opportunity only for it to be squandered. Do you understand that?'

'Yes, Mamma, I promise, I will practise really hard so you will be happy and proud of me.'

'Good. Very good. You will achieve great things and I will be proud of you.' Natalia resumed counting her money and turning the coins into neat piles.

Adi's first teacher, Signora Berta, was a cat-loving organist at the local church. She had six cats that wandered around the house and Natalia, who went to every lesson with Adi, found them distracting during lessons and to be an unprofessional aspect detrimental to the seriousness of the task so, after a year or two, she found what she considered a more appropriate teacher at the Conservatory of Music in Trieste: strict, serious, more expensive of course and singularly lacking cats. She and her environment were much more to Natalia's liking.

It was at this time, when Adi was five or six, that Natalia's cruel streak began to manifest itself even more as she took on with gusto a vicarious and demanding role. She wanted her daughter to progress quickly and faultlessly. A daughter of hers had to be special, perfect and perhaps, God willing, even a genius. She wanted to achieve by having her daughter achieve and was relentless in its pursuit. She sat in on all the lessons as well as all the practice sessions at home. There was rigid discipline. Mistakes were intolerable. Scales and arpeggios were repeated again and again until mastered; pieces practised until they were bound to impress the teacher to such an extent that the mother could bask in the praise directed at her daughter and thus, indirectly, at her. What's more, this teacher did not praise lightly. Her praise meant something, it was serious, not merely a means of propping up an ordinary student. That was very much to Natalia's liking: praise, not served on a platter, but earned the hard way.

Nothing short of excellence was tolerated. Wrong notes incurred Natalia's wrath but increasingly, her obsessive and wrathful vigilance extended to Adi's schoolwork as well. Schoolbooks were checked daily and red marks or lesser scores led to a degrading reprimand.

Eisteddfods were a particular nightmare for Adi. Natalia always insisted that they arrive early to secure a front row seat from which to scrutinise her daughter's performance in detail.

In time, it would be hard to imagine Adi not becoming increasingly anxious and fearful of her mother's uncompromising expectations. Even more than that, Adi would come to hate her because of the relentless pressure on her to be a prodigy. The issue of the mink coat would be raised again and again in the future as an illustration of how much her mother had sacrificed for an ungrateful, under-achieving daughter.

12

In the aftermath of the Second World War, Trieste teetered for a time atop the iron curtain dividing communist East and capitalist West, between Yugoslavia and Italy. For several years, it was uncertain which side would prevail and from 1947 to 1954, Trieste was declared a free territory under United Nations jurisdiction. Finally, in 1954, Trieste was returned to Italy, though much of the surrounding territory went to Yugoslavia.

In 1953, sensing that Italy would prevail, the family name was changed in an effort to become Italianised, from Kakovich to Cavini. Natalia also changed her maiden name from Regent to Reggente.

The changing of Guido's surname was in direct response to the ongoing regional tensions between Italians and Slavs and would have opened doors for Guido as he tried to secure a more prosperous career as a customs officer in Trieste. It would also have reduced the stigma their daughter faced at school and cleared some of the obstacles from her future path.

The decision, I have no doubt, would have been primarily my father's to make. As the sole breadwinner at the time, his career was important, and customs officers were relatively well paid. There was also the mouth-watering prospect of being regularly supplied with all those goods that, since the dawn of trade, found their way from the back of trucks to the family table. So the change of family name smoothed the transition from policeman to customs officer, but I have no doubt that Natalia, with her eyes forever on her daughter's future, welcomed the change also.

Why then the decision to emigrate barely two years later? Such a decision seems incompatible with the decisions made so far and the prospects that could be reasonably expected in Italy. The standard clichéd response is for a better life, for better opportunities for the children, as well as for the chance to own your own home. In many cases, these reasons may be the sole ones, but in the case of the Cavinis that simply cannot be. Why abandon a well-paid profession with good prospects to go to a country whose language one doesn't speak only to start all over again, most likely in a poorly paid menial job? Why fall back to the very bottom rung? Why leave family and friends? Why walk out of a beautiful home, albeit rented, in a comfortable middle-class suburb of Trieste to end up God knows where? What is the lie behind the photo depicting a united family striding confidently ahead, eyes fixed firmly on a certain future?

Guido was the driving force behind the decision to emigrate and, I now believe, it had nothing to do with a better life or home ownership and everything to do with punishing his wife.

'You'll be pleased to know I've got the tickets,' Guido told her sarcastically.

'Go to hell.'

'We sail for hell in July on a ship called *Flaminia*.' He went on flippantly, 'Did you know that she was originally an American ship? That's right, built in America and called *Missourian*. How about that, eh? They save us during the war only to sail us to hell.'

'You disgust me! I don't know how you can make a joke of everything, even of the misery you're inflicting on your own family.'

To Guido's mind, the punishment was thoroughly deserved. She'd cost him a son against his wishes. She'd had an affair with a cellist, and he had nagging doubts about it being ended. She had been willing to abandon her family for the cellist. Their marriage was in tatters. There was no love any more. They simply house-shared and job-shared. He had come to detest her controlling ways and the way she unrelentingly tormented their daughter. With divorce out of the question in Catholic Italy, he saw no alternative to going to the other side of the globe to start afresh.

Unlike Natalia, Guido felt no strong ties to family or friends in Italy and Slovenia, so what better way to punish her than to tear her away from everything and everyone she loved.

Guido coldly put the stark ultimatum to her. 'I'm going to Australia with my daughter. You can come if you like or you can stay here with your cellist and never see your daughter again. The choice is yours.'

It was an agonising decision Natalia was forced to make. Either way, her loss was unbearable. In the end, one can only surmise that being a mother carried most weight and that she really did love her daughter, in her own cool and conditional way, enough to sway her. I can imagine her mentally balancing the ledger into piles for and against, just as she liked to arrange money into neat piles, and deciding that she had already invested far too much of herself into her daughter to simply let it all go. She still had high hopes for Adi.

The entire episode must have seemed incredibly surreal. I think that until the actual day of departure Natalia could not quite believe that it was going to happen and perhaps even managed to convince herself that it wouldn't; that something, anything, would intervene to prevent it. But nothing intervened and, on that day, 16 July 1955, with her bravest countenance on display, she was borne along the dock by the merest thread and somehow managed to resist the urge to turn around with her daughter and run.

Natalia's family was there, her friends were there, none of them could believe it was actually happening, that this dreaded day had arrived, the day they were losing Natalia. Many cried, not knowing if they would ever see each other again. Guido's family was not there. Only his best friend Giordano and his wife Eta came to see them off.

That day was forever added to the lengthening list of Natalia's regrets. She blamed, and never forgave, her husband and daughter, no matter what they did to try to bring happiness and ease her burden. She never returned to Italy. Most of her family and friends never saw her again. Only her ashes made the journey back, to rest beside her mother in the cemetery at Contovello.

13

It was hot going through the Suez Canal. Arab merchants plied their wares whenever the ship stopped, their goods hauled up and the money lowered by rope.

For Adi, who had never been overseas, it was like being on an exotic holiday and her excitement was constant. Suddenly there were other kids to play with, there was a swimming pool and no piano lessons or schoolwork to do. The boxed-up piano was stowed in the cargo hold and forgotten. She could simply have fun.

For Guido, it was an adventure. Forever sanguine, the journey represented freshness; a fresh start for himself and his family, leaving all troubles behind boxed-up in place and in time. He made every effort too to have fun and let bygones be bygones. Each swell that the ship crashed through took them closer to the future, a brighter future, a simpler future, with just the three of them. Each wave produced another cleansing sweep of the slate.

For Natalia, this ridiculous feat of pure escapism simply brought on dread, emptiness, depression and seasickness. She saw not one positive aspect in it all; there was only loss.

During the crossing of the Indian Ocean, the sea became very rough and the ship sustained some damage and much of the passengers' cargo received varying degrees of water damage, including the Cavinis' piano. They spent a day in Colombo and three days in Fremantle, arriving on 14 August, where the ship underwent repairs.

I don't know what Fremantle was like back in 1955 – very working-class, I imagine – but to my family it must have been like another galaxy. They went out for a day to explore the town and stopped at a café for some lunch. They understood next to no English other than the little they had learned on the ship. Guido gestured for some food and they were shown to a table and handed a menu.

'What does all this mean?' he asked Natalia jokingly.

'Who knows?' she replied.

'Look! I see spaghetti!' Adi squealed with delight.

They were excited. They had not expected to see spaghetti on the menu of an eatery in this far-flung corner of the world as far from Italy as was imaginable. They could also see coffee. Suddenly the place seemed not quite as foreign, perhaps even hospitable. They ordered three spaghettis and two coffees, and managed to somehow get a lemonade for Adi. The food duly arrived and their hopeful illusions were shattered; it was tinned spaghetti on toast!

'What is this crap?' cried Guido.

'I've never seen anything like it,' replied Natalia in disgust.

Only Adi managed to finish her meal. She quite liked its sweetness. Natalia gagged as she tried to swallow the mush and Guido couldn't face a second mouthful. The coffee was no better – a milky swill that barely tasted of coffee at all.

Eventually, the waiter returned and asked if they wanted anything else.

'No, no, *basta*,' said Guido.

In their dialect, *basta* means enough, but the waiter, seeing two of the meals barely touched, thought he was being called a bastard and took exception. It took a lot of explaining to finally make the waiter understand that no offence was meant. It was the first time they heard the words dagos and wogs and had no idea what they meant, but in time, they would become very familiar.

They reached the port of Melbourne on 19 August. It was dark and cold. Having disembarked at Station Pier, they boarded a bus which took them to what was then Spencer Street Station, now Southern Cross. From there, a train took them to Albury, then another bus took them to the Bonegilla migrant centre, a collection of ex-army corrugated-iron barracks, which was to be their home for the next month.

Bonegilla migrant centre, 1955.

Some of the barracks are still there, part of an immigration museum, and it is a moving experience for those with a connection to walk amongst them and commune with the spirits still there.

They arrived at Bonegilla in the early morning, cold and exhausted. Once allocated to a building, they took what possessions they had with them and went straight to bed.

As part of the assisted passage program, they were to remain in Bonegilla until Guido received a job offer, the first that came along, which he couldn't refuse. It was midwinter, the place was cold and the food was terrible. They spoke of the nauseating stench of mutton fat and of the flavourless boiled vegetables that went with the meat. There were no sauces, there was no garlic, there were no condiments whatsoever. Everyone hated it.

To make things a little more pleasant and palatable, Guido made regular trips into Albury by bus to buy food and also a small cooking stove so they could cook and eat better. Then, once he'd landed a job at McKay's in Sunshine, a factory for making farm equipment, he made some trips to Melbourne to find accommodation suitable for himself and his family.

To Adi, nine years old at the time, leaving Trieste on a ship that was taking them halfway around the world to a new land had been an exciting adventure, but on that first morning at Bonegilla, she felt terrified. She found herself in a cold, windswept camp where miserable grey-looking people huddled around murmuring, trying to keep warm and trying to swallow food that wouldn't go down. Everything was totally foreign, but kids are kids no matter where they are, and she managed to team up with some and so, for some of the time at least, she was able to have some fun and to forget the things that worried her. The rest of the time, it was her father who reassured her. He took on the burden of doing what had to be done to make it more bearable for all of them, and he went about it in his typical uncomplaining manner.

Even to Guido, Bonegilla was a shock. He wasn't prepared for such an austere, barren, unwelcoming place and he felt acutely the burden of responsibility placed on his shoulders for his family being there. With that in mind, he did everything he could to make their stay there more comfortable. He maintained his confident, sanguine outlook and reassured both his wife and daughter that their stay would be a short one. To that end, he pestered the authorities to get him a job as soon as possible.

Natalia, as always, was enigmatic. She rarely spoke with me about her experience at Bonegilla and then only in the most simplistic terms such as the food being bad or the weather being cold or that they just lived like animals. I suspect she wanted to forget about the whole episode and, anyway, it was to be completely overshadowed by other events in due course and relegated to a triviality by comparison. Adi recalls her being stoic, solemn and keeping to herself most of the time. However, she did befriend another woman and they spent a lot of time knitting together and quietly conversing.

On sporadic occasions, she even managed to smile, such as on a trip to Hume Weir on a bright, sunny Albury day; but I'm sure, below the surface in her molten soul, in the words of the Trieste dialect, Triestino, she would have thought, *'Qua, Dio ga ditto basta.* Here, God has said enough.' She may have found a measure of comfort in thinking that these were surely the worst of times. In her wretchedness, some solace came from her belief that this was the bottom, that they could fall no further, and that from here their lives in the promised land must improve. But through a calamitous mix of misfortune and incompatible parts, that was not to be the case.

14

After a month of enduring Bonegilla, they moved to Melbourne. Guido began work at McKay's in Sunshine as a machinist on the production line, building farm implements, including the famous Sunshine Harvester which gave the suburb its name. They rented space in a house in Dulcie Street, Sunshine, and Natalia found a Catholic school for her daughter by going around with daughter in tow making the sign of the cross.

The house was a large and simple cement brick place owned by an Italian truckie. More importantly, it was cheap. The drawback was that they shared it with five other recently arrived European families! It was chaos. For a time, Guido, naturally gregarious, enjoyed the cosy camaraderie, Adi had other children to muck around with but for Natalia, right from day one, it was insufferable. For a woman of quiet dignity, natural elegance and colossal snobbishness, all these working-class people in such surroundings were far too common and beneath her. The other women in particular irritated her. They squabbled often as they fell over one another in the cramped conditions. After three months, Natalia was at the end of her tether; they moved.

The next place was in Fawkner Street, North Sunshine. At that time, it was a frontier suburb at the very edge of western Melbourne. Beyond their back fence were just paddocks. It was very quiet. They shared the house with the owners, a childless Sicilian couple, and it was so remote that Guido and the owner could jump the back fence and shoot rabbits for dinner. It was here in 1956 that Adi had her tenth birthday party and Natalia found work as a seamstress in Melbourne at quite a posh little business in Collins Street, the Three Little Tailors, that was very much to her liking. Her fairy's hands were productive once more, finally making the stylish garments that she was meant to.

They remained at Fawkner Street for a year and it was a good year, and when they eventually did move, it was to a house of their own in Miller's Road, Brooklyn.

Both Guido and Natalia continued to work and Adi attended Brooklyn State School, which was right across the road from their house. It was the first time in her life that she attended a secular school and she found it to her liking and liberating. There were no more nuns, prayers and religious education. She was happy there, but as always, the pressure applied by her mother to succeed was relentless regardless of the type of school.

Home ownership, the dream of so many, both native-born and migrant, is the holy grail. It is one of the crowning events of life. Our lives are broken into chapters according to where we live. It contributes in no small way to defining who we are, and is universally seen as a measure of success and status. But for Guido and Natalia this great milestone quickly soured.

It was all Guido's doing of course. Natalia was terrified of debt and preferred the tranquillity of a 'paid in full' life to a debtor's tormented one. I imagine that, yet again, her caution would have been swept aside by the tsunami of Guido's bombastic and untempered optimism and boundless trust in the goodwill of others. Guido's Achilles heel was that he took people at face value, always dealt fairly and openly, and expected others to do the same. The rest is the familiar story of too much borrowed, too much interest, repayments not met and, within a year, everything lost.

Natalia's fury can very easily be imagined. Her white-hot rage could have powered half a city and cowed an army of Vikings. Her screaming and her seething, shaking body would have rattled even the normally imperturbable Guido, just as it would have rattled the tectonic plate on which Brooklyn and their lost home sat. He had gone against her caution like a fool and was too willing to put his trust in strangers rather than her and now she was trapped by his failed grand plan. There was nowhere for her to go. She was stuck with this impossible man who had led her to this life of misery and toil far away from everyone she loved, and if that wasn't bad enough, now they were homeless and penniless and had to start again from scratch. It was difficult for all of them but for Natalia it was beyond a nightmare and surely this time things could not possibly get worse. They did.

Guido responded by doing what he always did in a crisis, he worked harder. To his work at McKay's he added labouring for a concreter and haircutting for anyone who wanted it. It brought in extra money but did not bring happiness.

It was at this time, around late 1957, that they moved to Waratah Street, West Footscray, number 20, which was to be the family home until it was sold shortly after Natalia's death in 1992. They bought the unfinished property cheap as it consisted solely of the frame and roof, with another couple. While both men worked to finish the house, the Cavinis lived in the bungalow at the back of the property and the other couple lived elsewhere. It took about a year to complete the job and then both couples moved into the house but once more it didn't take long for Natalia to get sick of the company. It took six months, in fact, for Natalia to get so thoroughly sick of the other woman that the other couple were bought out and the Cavinis had a home of their own again.

Other than being the family home, there was nothing particularly special about it. It was a boring, standard, weatherboard place of that period, painted mostly in drab grey with white trim, and yet one face of the house was painted bright yellow. It seems odd now, a two-tone home, but I thought nothing of it at the time. Perhaps it was the fashion then, like two-tone cars seemed to be for a while. Anyway, thinking about it now, it made the house look like it was three-quarters depressed and one-quarter manic, perhaps in a subconscious way reflecting Natalia's own mind.

But if the house itself was uninspiring, the block and the neighbourhood more than made up for it. It would come to be a child's paradise, a place to fire the imagination and to weave spells and dreams. The possibilities for play, adventure, exploration and destruction were limitless, and in time, full use would be made of all these virtues.

The block was triangular with an unusually long street frontage. On one side lived the neighbour we called 'Grongo', at number 18, with his wife. This unflattering epithet was Natalia's creation. She was typically disdainful of both of them, despite barely knowing them, because of what she perceived to be their ignorant, crude, almost savage natures. To my knowledge, the word has no meaning but it came to describe perfectly, to me at least, this mysterious neighbour I rarely saw, except for the odd glimpse over the paling fence, and almost never heard, apart from sporadic loud talk in a foreign tongue. He and his wife seemed to lurk in their perpetually dark house or in the dim forest floor of the unkempt jungle-like garden that surrounded it. Grongo always looked morose to me and his wife frail.

I was scared of him, terrified in fact, even though he had never done the slightest harm to me or to anyone else that I know of. The name was enough to scare me and the gloom of their property was sufficient to set me on edge. In my imagination, he was a child-killer, a monster, a caveman living in his dark cave in a forest from which he solely emerged to hunt and eat children.

There was no love for thy neighbour from our side, Natalia saw to it, although I don't think Guido minded him, in the same way that he pretty much didn't mind anyone. Grongo's crime, I guess, was merely to be base and ignorant in my mother's perpetually judgemental eye and that was sufficient to have him blacklisted. These were unforgivable traits to her and, as was the case more often than not, what she said on such matters went. I have no idea whether her judgement was right or wrong but Grongo and his wife would not have been tolerated in our house and, by the same token, their house would not have been suitable for us.

On the other side of our block was Stony Creek which, despite being little more than an industrial drain at the time, so much so that it seemed to flow a different colour every day, nevertheless was a liquid bounty of play to all the kids in the area. Across the creek was a huge paddock where horses were often grazed and at the top of which, bordering on Lae Street, was an old-fashioned playground with absolutely none of the present-day safety features. Added to this were the large number of large cypresses and willows along the creek, the massive tunnels under Geelong Road and the quarry that was where Hatfield Court is now. You can imagine the fun and adventures to be had. It was a great place and a great time to be a kid.

Guido continued to work at McKay's, soon to be taken over by Massey Ferguson, but now it was further to travel on his no-frills bicycle and he was forever getting punctures on the rough roads. The sight of his bicycle resting upside-down on the driveway undergoing repairs was a common one.

Natalia managed to get a job nearby, virtually at the top of the street, at a factory called Bramac on Geelong Road, where they made raincoats and other wet weather gear. It was a come-down from the Collins Street tailors which was made up for by the convenience of a five-minute walk to work. The windfall of time was spent on domestic duties and extra supervision of her daughter's studies.

Adi was back at a Catholic school and not particularly overjoyed about it. She went to the local Catholic school at Corpus Christi, which was also well within walking distance on Ormond Road, just off Geelong Road. It was also the church they attended to celebrate mass and special religious occasions.

Both parents were working, sufficient money was coming in, they had a home of their own, Adi was doing well at school and the piano and they were all in good health. A fair measure of stability had finally been achieved so the time was rapidly approaching for the next step.

15

The early years at Waratah Street both before my birth and for a short period after were without doubt the happiest years for the Cavini family in Australia. Their fortunes waxed. There were good times. There were happy weekends spent in the garden, on improvements to the house or on outings to the beach, picnics or movies. For Guido, only one thing remained to be done and on that he had his daughter's wholehearted support: the completion of his family.

The stumbling block of course would be his wife, the future mother of his second child. Convincing her would take some doing and, without his daughter's backing, would have been nigh on impossible. He was well aware that his own desires did not rate highly, but those of Adi did carry some weight where it mattered most. He put his faith and his hope in the belief that eventually two against one would prevail even though that one held all the important cards.

He anticipated Natalia's resistance. He knew what she would say. Work, income, independence, home, achievement. These were all important to her and another baby would change all that; and they weren't getting any younger – she was thirty-seven, he was thirty-nine. Life was good, they were secure. Why put all that at risk? He understood how she would react and braced himself for it. He even accepted that at their age it was perhaps folly, but the urge would not leave him. To Guido, the family was incomplete, Adi deserved and wanted a sibling, he wanted a son, she wanted a sister but, perhaps on a more fundamental level, I think that Guido saw no real point to anything they were doing without having another child to do it for.

The three were finishing their dinner, *risi con fungi*, mushroom risotto in our dialect, simple and flavoursome food as always, with a large green salad that Guido always insisted on to accompany it. As soon as they'd sat down, Natalia sensed that something was afoot and that they were both in on it. It was absolutely impossible to pull wool, or anything else for that matter, over her eyes. She observed some agitation. Guido seemed awkward. He kept trying to refill her wine glass despite her declining twice. Adi moved in her seat more than usual. She also felt that she had a pretty good idea what it was all about. There had been rumblings before and, unbeknown to them, she had given the matter some private thought and was now inclined to go along with the whole business. But she was not about to let on; she enjoyed watching each of them working themselves into a good lather. It amused her to see how terrified they were of broaching the subject. She enjoyed watching them squirm. She had to restrain herself from laughing aloud at this cowardly pair, frightened of a diminutive woman – albeit, even she had to admit, a diminutive woman with an uncompromising mind and a rather sharp tongue.

Natalia made to leave the table with an air of disgust after refusing Guido's third offer of more wine.

'Please sit,' he said.

'I've had sufficient,' she innocently replied.

'I want to talk.'

'Oh! What about?'

'Me too, Mamma, I want to talk too. I want a baby sister, well, even a baby brother would do, any baby really, and only you can give us one.'

'Oh, that.'

'Yes, that,' said Guido, with the tone of one totally usurped.

'Please, Mamma, please, I really want a baby. I'll look after it and help you as much as I can and I'll spoil it and play with it and feed it and dress it and do everything. I don't know where you go to get babies but I'll help you with that too if you tell me how. Please, Mamma, I'll do anything…'

Adi's plea was cut short by her parents' explosive laughter. Her passion gave way to indignation which in turn gave way to joyous satisfaction as it dawned on her that their prolonged united laughter represented victory. She immediately felt the heady climax of a done deal. She would get her sister; even a brother would be better than nothing.

Thus, somewhere in the latter stages of 1958, the process began, a husband's task was duly completed and it was left to the wife to finish the job.

I was born early on a Wednesday morning on 12 August 1959 at the Footscray and District Hospital. I was keen to get out, arriving four weeks premature. The birth was difficult; Natalia lost a lot of blood, which heralded an anaemic indolence from which she never entirely recovered. Physically exhausted by the ordeal, there followed a pallor and frailty that defined her post-natal period and beyond.

There is a photo of me taken when I was around two weeks old. It is taken outside in the front garden and I am in a bundle of blankets that seems to be ten times my size. My head is to one side and it appears that I am asleep. The garden, like any new garden, is sparse. The entire street, or what little of it that is visible, also looks bare, with only a few trees visible and starkly prominent power poles punctuating the background. I am in my mother's arms as she is sitting on the brick retaining wall which ran along the length of the front picket fence. Her thick dark hair is magnificent and her attire, as always, is perfectly neat and modest. With her rounded white collar, she could almost be taken for a virtuous schoolgirl. She is holding her new offspring in both arms, her right hand also clutching a small bunch of flowers. Her hands are small and delicate. It is the last photo taken of her while she still enjoyed relatively good health. She is smiling, and her pretty, rounded face looks happy; but she wasn't. Following my birth, her physical and mental health deteriorated.

Guido was happy. In fact, he was delighted. He had his son, he had one of each, his family was complete. He had a secure job where he was respected. They had a roof over their heads which they owned. Everything he wanted from life had come to fruition, fully vindicating his decision to emigrate.

Adi was ecstatic. If she was at all disappointed at not having a sister, it was short-lived and her motherly doting over her little brother began on day one and continues to this day.

Natalia struggled in the immediate post-natal period from fatigue, anaemia and the shackles of depression. To her mind, once more, she was the one forced to suffer so as to bring joy to others. She was the one paying the price to give others what they wanted.

(As an interesting aside, and an extraordinary coincidence, the midwife at my birth, Maureen, was the aunt of my future wife and she and Natalia would briefly reunite some thirty years later.)

But in time, Natalia came through the baby blues. Indefatigable as always, she bought an industrial sewing machine so she could work from home while raising a child. In no time at all, she landed a contract supplying clothes to a business in Richmond run by a Jewish family. Natalia, for a time, was relatively content, or as content as it was possible for her to be, so it followed, as night follows day, that everyone else was content too. She carried on stoically: running a household, raising a daughter and a baby as well as sewing to earn some money and to keep her career flickering. But she had never been physically strong and now it seemed to be harder than ever for her to find the energy required to simply get through another day.

In time, her strength abandoned her. Every day was a struggle. Adi arrived from school to untidiness and unfinished jobs. Guido arrived from work to a dinnerless kitchen. Husband and daughter worried. Something wasn't quite right.

About six months after my birth, the pains began in Natalia's neck, wrists, hands and knees. The pain was unrelenting and distressing. It was even worse at night, so that she couldn't sleep, adding to her exhaustion. Her joints would swell and seize and it wasn't long before she could no longer sew. She struggled to do anything at all. The family worried.

Natalia went to her local general practitioner, Dr Poutsma, whose clinic was close by on Geelong Road. His tests confirmed his suspicions, that Natalia had rheumatoid arthritis. He treated her with aspirin – there was virtually no other treatment available at that time – which eased the pain and stiffness a little but did nothing to alter the disease process itself. Her rheumatoid arthritis was particularly aggressive and within a short time she was referred to the rheumatology outpatient clinic at Footscray Hospital, run by Dr Mathews, where she had more blood tests, and X-rays, and ended up with larger brown-glass jars of aspirin and bottles of Mylanta. This was also where she was introduced to her lifelong friend and enemy prednisolone, the two-faced drug.

This stage marked the end of Natalia as my father and sister had known her and the beginning of the only Natalia that I was to know. It was to be a miserable thirty-two-year journey of decay for her and for those around her. A life destroyed but still lived. A struggle against chronic pain, disability and indignity. A fight against shame, bitterness, disappointment and futility. There followed every step of the way a mental disintegration. Natalia became vicious, depressed, paranoid and full of self-loathing while also loathing those who tried to help her the most – her own family. Blame was readily apportioned. The depth of her feeling of worthlessness and uselessness were very evident; she despised herself as well as those she judged to be responsible for her predicament.

Chief among those was of course Guido, who not only could never have been said to be her true love, but also, by his ultimatum, was the key instrument of her demise. His action carved her from family, friends, security and a future; tore her mercilessly from a love of true kindreds and dumped her in a place where she felt no connection with anything or anyone. Finally, she firmly believed, his insistence on another child directly led to her physical destruction. She had been so weakened, that the rheumatoid arthritis could take hold. All this she could never, ever forgive.

Adi, of course, was also culpable. She was never quite good enough, a constant source of strain and irritation, and it was for her daughter that Natalia had given up so much, made such a sacrifice, spent so much money and come to this soulless country. All this she would never, ever forget and would come to expect in return nothing short of complete devotion, self-sacrifice and indentured servitude.

I didn't escape her wrath either. Once my sister left home, the duties and chores fell to me and as Natalia became more and more disabled and her needs increased, my workload increased. But I was never the object of hate that Guido and Adi were. I was, after all, innocent of past events. With me, it was more subtle. I was not subjected to her hatred but neither was I bestowed a mother's love.

There was the expectation that I had to help my mother, of course, and being essentially a placid, introverted child, I did what had to be done for her with very little complaint. This was all reinforced by the notion she instilled in me that it was her and me against them, Guido and Adi, as well as practically everyone else on the planet who didn't care for either of us. However, there were some undertones of blame directed at me which became more apparent as I got older and the basis of which was that she had done so much for me, sacrificed so much and that my birth had led inexorably to her tragic illness. Self-pity and guilt were weapons she wielded with great skill whenever she sensed subservience wain.

'Look at me, look at what I have become, look at what they have done to me, look at what you have done to me. Me and you, no one else, us against them, those evil thieves who have taken everything from me. I wish God would take me.'

That was the sort of thing she would say to me. She was, above all, a masterful manipulator.

16

There is no treason like the treason of autoimmune disease. It comes in many guises but all have the common purpose of turning the body's own antibodies against itself in a macabre course of self-destruction. There is no other purpose and the traitor responsible is one's own immune system. It harbours no mercy, compassion or malice. It displays a psychopathic lack of empathy but it is not vengeful, it is merely mistaken. Its weapons of choice are deranged antibodies that fulfil their duty without question, emotion and with virtually no hope of armistice. What brings all this about remains largely a mystery. There is no grand plot or conspiracy, no clandestine meetings, no discussion of strategy or tactics in hushed tones in darkened drawing rooms. The renegade simply takes it upon itself to wreak havoc on an unsuspecting and completely innocent host, in what is an undeclared state of civil war.

Nowadays, there are very effective weapons available to the host to fight back. Some collateral damage invariably occurs and complete victory is never assured, unconditional surrender is rarely possible, but a stalemate can be virtually guaranteed. Back in the 1960s, this was not the case. The weapons were crude and unsuited to precise and effective counter-attack. The host invariably capitulated to a greater or lesser extent.

I remember Natalia coming home from hospital with those huge brown-tinted glass bottles of aspirin with a screw-on lid and a wide neck stuffed with cottonwool. For a long time that was it, that was all she had to fight with. It helped a little with the symptoms but in no way impeded the juggernaut's all-conquering march. Later came newer anti-inflammatories such as phenylbutazone and indomethacin, which again provided symptom relief but no long-term benefit. There were gold injections, dumb bombs that hit or missed; they didn't work in Natalia's case. What did work was corticosteroid, either injected into the worst affected joints or taken orally as prednisolone. The prednisolone, at sufficient dose, could stop the traitor in its tracks, but each victory was pyrrhic; the long-term cost in the form of side-effects could be enormous and in Natalia's case it was.

When you find yourself gradually becoming crippled, when your life and the essence of who you are is being taken from you, when you are ravaged by severe pain day and night from which there is little reprieve, when nothing else seems to help, then you will try anything. There was prayer, massage, natural therapies, therapeutic mud baths somewhere in Kew; nothing worked, nothing except for the deal done with the devil, prednisolone. It alone provided rapid symptom relief and a slowing or cessation of the disease process itself but it came at a frightful long-term cost which included weight gain, diabetes, hypertension, skin and muscle wasting, increased susceptibility to infection and osteoporosis. The trick was to find the lowest dose that would do the job.

Eventually, Natalia could barely move her neck at all. She had to pivot her entire back to see to the sides. Her elbows looked as if they could simply fall apart at any moment. Her wrists were boggy and deformed with synovial swelling. Her knees were also swollen and had no strength. But nothing shocked or epitomised her condition like the state of her hands. The knuckles were swollen and her fingers were swept to one side like wheat in a gale, the so-called ulnar deviation, and there were all manner of other deformities due to a combination of joint and tendon destruction. There was no strength in her fingers. She could barely grip at all, they were good for nothing, they simply flopped around at the knuckle like limp fish. The hands of a fairy were no more. Her bones became brittle, all of her muscles wasted away to feeble floppy flesh, her teeth succumbed to gingivitis, her skin was frail and pasty, she bruised for no reason at all and her face took on the telltale shape of the moon.

The longer Natalia suffered, the longer we all did. With each year, she became more cruel, more bitter and more vicious. The voids in her mind, which naturally developed with inactivity, were filled with paranoid and deluded thoughts so that she came to trust no one and suspected everyone, and in the end her mental demons were the equal of her physical ones.

Natalia, at Waratah Street, 1964.

17

I peeled two oranges, one for my mother and the other for me. It was no longer possible for her to do it. It was impossible for her to do just about anything these days. She liked to read and do crosswords. She sang and liked Tom Jones and was an admirer of Billy Graham but hated President Johnson. From a young age, she taught me how to use the sewing machine. The chores were left to me and there was always plenty to do.

We ate the oranges and then we played draughts. It was always either draughts or cards. She was quite good at both but her hands struggled with the task of holding cards or moving pieces. I thought nothing much of it at the time; it was simply how her hands were. I felt no sympathy or disdain as she struggled to play and even to grip the orange and bring it to her mouth. Often, I put the orange in her mouth for her. I was eight or nine at the time and devoid of much feeling. It is hindsight which has given me the ability to feel sympathy.

Invariably, she would talk and I would listen, often about politics and what was happening in the news.

'The Americans have no business in Vietnam. They kill innocent people for big profits.'

This was her typical simplistic view of the world; anything America did was bad and motivated by profit, anything communists did was good and motivated by the well-being of workers. I naturally agreed with her that America and capitalism are evil and founded on greed while communists fight for the poor and the powerless. I was too young to think independently. I accepted whatever she told me as the truth.

Natalia worried about the Vietnam War all the time. She worried that if it dragged on, I could be drafted into the army and my life put at risk. Where would she be if I died or was seriously injured? Who would care for her?

Natalia's relationship with Guido deteriorated beyond repair. He was not welcome in what she saw as her domain. Guido worked long hours and spent little time at home. They avoided one another. Natalia also severed links with her daughter. Adi left home at age twenty-two after a litany of arguments. That left no one else at that time to care for her but me. Natalia told me that my father and sister had abandoned her, and by extension me, and I believed her. Why wouldn't I?

'Americans are greedy,' she went on. 'I saw them in Trieste with all their money and loose ways. All they respect is money.'

She despised the coarse ways and arrogance of the average GI despite the fact that they were largely responsible for liberating Western Europe at great cost. While she focused on America, I focused on the game, chalked up another win, and only then attended to disliking Americans.

Natalia loved to sing. She had a strong voice; the only part of her that was still strong. I didn't appreciate it at the time for I had no particular liking for music, not the type she sang anyway. She sang Italian songs, Russian songs, German songs; often national anthems sung in stirring tones. She would sing moving songs about mothers, and fathers. The songs she sang about America were in mocking tones that reflected her own anti-imperial and anti-capitalist dogma intensified by events in Vietnam. The entire world was critical of the US at the time – her enemies, her allies and most notably, a large portion of her own citizens. More curious was Natalia's attitude towards Great Britain and the former British empire, which was barely of any relevance any longer. Nevertheless, she would blast out 'God Save the Queen', 'Rule Britannia' and 'Land of Hope and Glory' with such sardonic gusto that I would join in, thus forming a bizarre duet devoted to mocking British tradition and glory. It was all quite bizarre. She also mocked the British monarchy while at the same time being completely fascinated by their goings-on.

Much of her attitude was to do with her leftist ideology that I automatically embraced. She threw America and Britain into the same pot: capitalist greed, obsession with profit and exploitation of weaker nations and peoples. She was as blind to any of their virtues as she was to the possibility of any evil-doing in the communist world, and she wasn't alone. It was the norm amongst naive intellectuals at the time and she liked to think of herself as an intellectual with a sharp mind and an equally sharp tongue that saw her prevail ninety-nine times out of a hundred in an argument.

Like many intelligent, free-thinking, left-leaning people, she had feelings of not so much grandeur as of superiority. She imparted that sense of being somehow special onto her children. She would say we weren't standard – in other words, not out of the common stock. She felt she had superior intellect and moral values to those around her. She treated what she considered common people with disdain and condescension in much the same way that leftist manifestos refer to the 'masses'. She was a devotee of Marx and Lenin, but I know that she was appalled by the atrocities carried out by Stalin and did not share the view of other communist sympathisers that what Stalin did were necessary evils for the greater good; the rooting out of reactionary beliefs that would otherwise harm the welfare of the masses.

Another leftist cause which she adopted wholeheartedly was support for the PLO against Israel. In fact, in common with a lot of Europeans at the time, and despite the ravages of the Holocaust, she was anti-Semitic, and supported any Arab cause against Israel. Israel was seen merely as a greedy capitalist spin-off of America stolen from the Palestinians. Needless to say, she also backed Mao and Castro, no matter what atrocities were committed against their own people.

More disturbing still was the attitude of Natalia, and more so some of her contemporaries, towards Germany. There seemed to be a respect and even admiration for all things German. Their discipline, ingenuity and workmanship were legendary. Natalia sang the German national anthem with reverence, as though two world wars were merely a hiccup, the teething pains of a young nation blessed with culture and greatness.

But it was the attitude of some of our acquaintances, men and women, that was particularly unnerving. Discussing their grievances with the modern world and bemoaning the ways of youth, on more than one occasion I heard, to the accompaniment of nodding and murmurs of agreement, that what the world needed was another Hitler. They seemed to be only half joking, if at all. Anti-Semitism seemed the norm when I was a kid and also as a counter to the new hippie culture with the perceived breakdown of social morality that went with it in the form of drugs, promiscuity, the pill, long hair, short skirts and devil's music; they pined for discipline, order and a return of respect for family and religion and an end to the soft, self-indulgent and rebellious liberal ideas of youth. They wanted Hitler's social cleansing and uniformity of belief. They wanted strength, someone who would crush the new ways, however misguided.

Mussolini, on the other hand, seemed to be generally considered a fool, with delusions of grandeur about becoming a modern-day Roman emperor by conquering a few minnows. He was a stain on the pride of Italy who deserved his fate.

Needless to say, Natalia always supported the ALP and for much of my life so have I. Back in the sixties and early seventies, things seemed politically more clear-cut. It was the ALP that offered an immediate end to Australia's participation in the Vietnam War, a break from blindly following the USA, social reforms, equal opportunity and access to free tertiary education based on merit rather than wealth and privilege. These were important initiatives to Natalia generally but also specifically for what they meant for me. They meant not only the end of young men being drafted but also young people from working-class backgrounds having a more equal chance through higher education. The ascension of Whitlam to power in 1972 saw these things come to fruition and I still feel indebted to the great man for the opportunities I would otherwise never have had.

We finished a second game of draughts which I also won. I packed up the game and cleared away the orange peel. Natalia wanted to go to the toilet and then back to bed. I helped her walk by holding her left upper arm. In her right hand she carried a walking stick but it wasn't of much use other than to steady her a little. I helped her to the toilet then, once in bed, I raised her legs and covered her with the bedding. She would read or do crosswords for a while before falling asleep.

18

Adi left home in 1968 when she was twenty-two and I was about to turn nine. She left because she'd finally had enough. She stayed on to help her mother as much as she could but it was a thankless task. To live with her only brought enmity. Nothing was ever good enough, Natalia's judgement was harsh, gratitude and appreciation virtually non-existent. Adi also stuck it out for as long as she could for my sake, knowing the burden that would fall on me once she left. The final straw came with Natalia's complete rejection of Adi's first serious boyfriend, a Pole named Michael. After just one or two meetings with him, she pronounced him unsuitable and in essence banished him from the home. The banishment was to be enforced by Guido as a means of keeping the peace with his wife. Guido and Michael had an argument instigated by Natalia's demand that Michael leave immediately and never return. He did leave, but took Adi with him.

Even at twenty-two, Adi felt immense guilt over abandoning the family, but in the end she could take no more. She was away for over a year, including ten months spent in Sydney, living in Balmain, and in all that time the guilt never left her. She exchanged letters with her father and with me. However, her letters and phone calls to her mother went unanswered.

Natalia always felt the need to be in complete control of any situation but in most respects she was no longer in control, and with each year that passed, her level of control diminished as her illness and reduced mobility worsened. In her own mind, she saw betrayal at all points of the compass. The reality was that her family did everything it could possibly do for her, she just didn't see it that way. Ironically, what she feared most was the destruction of the family unit, yet no one did more to bring that about than herself, through her own actions. The catalyst on this occasion was Michael but it could have been anyone, anyone who destabilised her situation, anyone who threatened to separate daughter from mother. Her futile attempt to prevent it merely accelerated it.

Yet another low point was reached in 1971. Adi and Michael were making plans to marry. They spent about six months, with Guido, renovating the bungalow at the back of our place so they could live there until they'd saved enough for a place of their own. This was only possible of course with Natalia's approval, which she duly gave, but with Natalia there could never be absolute certainty. Her word was changeable, almost worthless. On a whim, she would make solid ground dissipate, foundations disintegrate and cast-iron evaporate. It was one of the games she played.

Once the renovation was completed, Adi and Michael prepared to move in but Adi felt uneasy. So far, everything had gone too smoothly. This was not the norm whenever arrangements were made with her mother. At no time did Adi take a favourable outcome for granted, so she was angry and disgusted rather than surprised when at the last moment Natalia reneged on the arrangement. It was yet another act of spite perpetrated by a bitter woman who could be totally vile and I now believe that it was her intention all along.

I remember little of this actual event. I remember the bungalow being worked on and the transformation it underwent from a clapped-out plaything to something habitable. It seemed to be a happy time with work being done together for a purpose but the happiness and the togetherness were aberrations. I remember lots of sunny days with the sun shining in through the louvre windows and watching my father work and helping him when I could. The old cement sheeting was torn down and replaced by weatherboards outside and Masonite inside and next came the smell of fresh paint, a smell that seems to mark significant periods of our lives like no other.

The reneging changed everything. Guido was furious and even he had finally had enough. He separated from Natalia and left the family home never to return. For a couple of years, he lived in the bungalow, to stay close to me, but it was never a long-term option as it didn't have its own bathroom or toilet. He intended to use the facilities in the house but Natalia refused him entry, so he had to shower at work, piss under the lemon tree and shit into a bucket.

For my part, my loyalty to my mother did not waver. She must have had her own very good reasons for acting in the way she had that I did not question. The entire sorry episode reinforced in my mind the us-against-them dogma that she perpetuated.

Adi and Michael married on 18 September 1971. It was a quiet affair at the registry office in Melbourne attended only by immediate family. Natalia was the exception – she refused to go.

Once married, they lived with Michael's parents in West Footscray. It was to be another turbulent experience, in large part due to the machinations of a troublesome, meddling matriarch as well as her violent son. It took only three months for Adi to realise that the marriage was a mistake because of Michael's reluctance to stand up to his mother, his gambling and his rage. The situation became so bad for Adi that even a return home to live once more with her mother seemed preferable, but Michael retaliated by throwing their goldfish onto the road and threatening to shoot their cat with a speargun if she left!

At this point, I should say something about the role of religion in our lives. The fact that Adi and Michael chose a secular marriage is revealing. Both nominally Catholic, they turned their backs on one of the seven sacraments for the expressed purpose of having a small, quiet, no nonsense wedding. However, though I cannot speak for Michael, the decision went to the deeper question of faith.

There was even back then within our family what can only be described as hypocritical ambivalence towards God and religion. In terms of religion, it was one thing to be seen to be doing what was right and one's accepted duty in public – indeed, the pressure to do so in the Italian community at least was immense – but what was expressed and how one acted in private was an entirely different matter. Natalia had no time for religion other than for the keeping up of appearances. Ironically, for someone who despised such a large portion of humanity, one of her fundamental motivating forces was the opinion of others. I never saw her pray in private. Her faith in a benevolent God, if she had ever had it, seemed to have vanished. She felt abandoned by God. She said this many times through her long, miserable and undeserved illness. *'Dio me ga abandonna.'* I heard her pleas to God to take her from this life so often that they no longer had any effect on me and, whether or not He played a role in her death, her eventual passing according to her own expressed wishes was most belated.

Guido, on the other hand, seemed entirely indifferent to both God and religion. I never heard him ask anything of God even during his terminal illness. He disliked the common hypocritical practice of turning to God only *in extremis.* He expressed to Adi a wish to be able to have another five years of life, to enjoy the simple things in his retirement, but by and large he accepted his fate. I think that he was probably an atheist but we never spoke of such things. Nevertheless, he lived a good and, one could say, Christian life. He worked hard, was devoted to his family and never hurt anyone.

With respect to the church, both Guido and Natalia rather unkindly described priests as money-grubbing drunks. They spoke of so-and-so always having a red nose on account of excessive drink and such-and-such doing nothing but count money all day and that all the money would go to enhancing the riches of the Vatican. They ridiculed the passing around of the plate and were always critical of the Catholic church's wealth.

As a family, we went to church irregularly, less so the older I became, and finally not at all except for occasional important events. I was baptised of course, did my first communion, but I was never confirmed. The waning of faith is evident by the fact that Adi almost always attended Catholic schools whereas I attended only secular ones.

Naturally, all of this influenced the way Adi and I thought about church. It galled us that our parents expected us to go to church but wouldn't go themselves. As a child, mass bored me to tears, and I'm sure Adi felt the same, so instead of going to church as we were supposed to, we took to going for walks instead and once Adi obtained her driver's licence our horizon immediately broadened. Usually, we would drive to St Kilda to get a gelato at Leo's or, when Michael came along, I would be relegated to the back seat and we'd park somewhere around Albert Park Lake, where I'd have to watch those two going at it in the front bench seat of his Falcon 500 and count how many times they kissed. All this, while we were meant to be in the house of the Lord, surely meant that the pearly gates would be forever padlocked to all of us.

It was no real surprise therefore that Adi and Michael chose to wed at the registry office. Faith and the church played no significant part in our lives. It must have caused some disquiet amongst some friends and relatives, but I was not aware of it at the time. However, what may seem to be the act of an apostate, of betrayal, may also be seen as an act of deep respect for God and His principles when perceived in this light: Adi was already with child. To this day, Adi still attends mass every Christmas and Easter. Her faith in God is both ambivalent but also deeply ingrained and mostly covert. Her insolent attitude to the church, however, has certainly worsened over the years as more and more evil acts are exposed, perpetrated by so-called men of God. As for many others, long-standing respect for the church and its representatives has been replaced by deep disgust and disillusionment.

19

As is often the case, the act of becoming a mother brought mother and daughter closer together. Natalia was delighted with the birth of a grandson, Jason. It gave Natalia and Adi a commonality and grounds for a reconciliation, at least in part. There was never total trust on either part and the slate, muddied by the fiasco of the bungalow and other things, had by no means been completely wiped clean. But there was for now at least some joy, which provided respite from Natalia's self-centred and never-ending woes.

For Adi, it was a difficult time. She, Michael and babe were living with the in-laws and there was constant interference from the 'mother-in-law who always knows best', to the extent that she virtually took over the care of the baby. It was Natalia who resolved the situation to some extent when, on a visit there, she gave Dusia, a stern, stout Ukrainian, a good dressing down. Natalia asked Adi to bring the baby to her but Dusia quickly intervened, saying the baby was asleep and should not be disturbed. Everyone could hear Jason babbling in the distance, so he was clearly not asleep. Natalia demanded to see the baby and told Dusia that she had no right to interfere, that Adi was the mother and that she got to decide. Natalia had the backing of everyone else there, including Dusia's long-suffering husband Jan, so she was forced into a humiliating backdown.

This was another example of Natalia's fierceness whenever her family was threatened yet, tragically, she was at her most fierce against her family.

My sister was gone, busy now with her own family, and I saw less and less of my father. True, he was sleeping in the bungalow, but my loyalty was firmly with my mother, so I disliked him and avoided him.

Sensing my antagonism, and I'm sure well aware of the reason for it, he was filled with despair. Our relationship completely fell apart. He spent his free time with his daughter, or with friends, where he was warmly welcomed; and he realised that as far as I was concerned all he could do was wait.

We, my mother and I, became isolated and insular. Natalia did not like me going out, she did not like me having friends over and, although the birth of Jason made visits by Adi more pleasant and frequent, she didn't like me visiting my sister or my father. The old tensions remained. Christmas get-togethers were awkward, nightmarish affairs and I was glad when they were over.

Natalia actively undermined Guido and Adi at every turn, accusing them of all manner of things, including abandonment, selfishness and theft. I came to dislike my father and sister as one would dislike a pair of plotting traitors who meant us only harm when we had done nothing to deserve it.

Natalia's undermining was self-serving of course. It fuelled her self-pity and preserved and strengthened our unity; a unity that was crucial to her. I think I loved my mother. I did feel as if she had been abandoned by everyone and I didn't understand the reasons for that; I thought, incorrectly, that it was purely out of spite. I think I did feel sorry for my mother also – how could you not? – although I do not recall ever being in tune with my emotions to that extent. Things were simply as they were and it fell to me to care for her and I did it all out of a precocious sense of devotion and duty; perhaps love too. I admit to feeling some pride. I was doing things, albeit mostly just mundane domestic tasks, that adults would normally do. We were managing in spite of everything, on our own. I developed resilience and a strong sense of responsibility. It simply came down to the fact that there was so much to do, so much that had to be done, and no one else to do it.

At some stage, I began to sleep in my mother's bed in case she needed me during the night. I think I was aged ten or eleven. She usually needed help with toileting at night; but it was also about companionship, overcoming loneliness and warmth, perhaps even a manifestation of love and interdependence. She had no one else and, other than a couple of friends who were never welcome in the home, I had no one else. It certainly cemented our bond and reinforced the notion in my mind that there was no one else I could trust but I can still recollect some murmurings emanating from within me that it wasn't quite the right thing to do at my age, that it was perhaps even weird. I dismissed these toxic thoughts as best I could but they never entirely went away and I certainly knew well enough not to tell anyone that I slept with my mother. At the time, it seemed right and it served a purpose. It was better than being alone.

Unfortunately, I was a bed-wetter,which complicated the arrangement. I had always been told by both my mother and father that it was due to my laziness, as if I deliberately stayed in bed and wet myself because I couldn't be bothered getting up out of a warm bed to go to the toilet. This was said out of anger and was absurd but because it was repeated so often the accusation has always stayed with me and I have felt its presence many times in my life, spurring me on to work hard and harder still, in an equally absurd effort to disprove it.

Natalia would be very cross when she woke during the night to a wet patch of bed next to her, necessitating the changing of sheets and all the turmoil that went with it at some ridiculous hour. I can understand that – it was a pain for me too – but the humiliation, although somewhat lessened with time, was horrible. Once I was fully awake, I had to help Natalia out of bed into a chair, change the sheets and make the bed, get Natalia back into a cold bed and of course later that day I had to wash the sheets, hang them out to dry, then bring them in, fold them and put them away. It meant a lot of extra work I didn't need, but I couldn't stop the bed-wetting.

I washed all of our clothes – Natalia couldn't do any of it – and washing clothes back then was not as simple as nowadays. Our laundry was outside, between the bungalow and the old outdoor dunny, which incidentally was no longer in use now that we had proper sewerage and an indoor flush toilet. It had been one of those bucket-type dunnies, much to Natalia's disgust, which required manual emptying. I really felt sorry for the men the gruesome task fell to, particularly on one occasion when our mongrel dog Laddie broke his chain and had a go at one of them while he lugged the bucket towards the truck. We heard a lot of swearing and unfortunately some of the contents of the bucket ended up on the man and just about everywhere else. Some days later, we received a letter from Footscray Council that our buckets would no longer be emptied unless our dog was properly restrained. Fair enough too. I don't know that it would be much consolation to the unfortunate man to know that his misfortune gave my parents a rare cause for hearty laughter.

The laundry was simply built of cement sheeting and I remember many of the internal walls being covered in writing, arithmetic and times tables written by Adi in her old student days. It had power but no running hot water. The water for washing had to be heated in what we called 'the copper', basically a receptacle made of copper that probably held around a hundred litres of water. It had a firebox underneath for heating the water, which could then be transferred to the washing machine by bucket. The washing machine was one of those old wringer-types that agitated the clothes and then it was a matter of transferring the clothes manually through the wringer rolls and into the concrete tubs for rinsing in clean water before passing them through the wringer again and into the basket to be taken out to hang on the Hill's hoist to dry. It was quite a process and time-consuming too. The wringers used to drive me insane because they were forever getting clogged and springing loose, especially with larger items. It took a bit of work to caress items through them without a mishap and there passed many frustrating moments in that laundry with the poor old Westinghouse bearing the brunt of innumerable screams, kicks and beatings.

Natalia couldn't iron either, so I did that too. Not that there was generally much of it to be done. She spent most of her time in pyjamas and a dressing gown and I generally wore clothes straight off the line.

I got away with being a bed-wetter. None of my friends or school colleagues ever found out. It is a relief to me even to this day. The embarrassment of being found out would have been unendurable. I hope the stigma associated with enuresis has lessened in these more open and supposedly tolerant times because the fear of discovery and the connotation of being a sissy and being ostracised as a result has the potential to cause great psychological harm to kids.

I continued to suffer with enuresis sporadically until I was thirteen, when it finally stopped. It was around that time that I moved back into my own bed in my own bedroom. The realisation that I was growing up, reinforced by the cessation of bed-wetting, now made it imperative; but there was also another reason, an incident from that time which continues to disturb me. I often snuggled up to Natalia in bed for warmth or comfort, an act which was never unwelcomed by her. If she thought I had wet the bed, she would feel the sheets or my pyjamas for wetness. On one occasion, she felt my pyjamas between my legs and it seemed at the time that her hand remained there longer than was necessary merely to detect wetness. I could be wrong, I hope I am, it may have been entirely accidental, but the doubt has stayed with me and I will never know for certain.

For the most part during that time, my mother and I got on quite well. Generally, I did as I was told. I accepted life as it was, I accepted that my mother was not like other mothers, I accepted that she was disabled and needed help with everything. We did get some help. We had a lady from the council that came once a week to do some of the cleaning and shopping, but very few of them ever impressed my mother with the standard of their work. It was impossible to meet my mother's meticulous standards in the time allotted to them. Doing things right, exactly as she wanted, fell onto my little shoulders. There was also a district nurse who came twice a week to bath her and to monitor her health and how we were managing.

There is a particular incident that distresses me probably more than any other from that time. It is true that I felt some unease when it occurred but not unduly; it was an incident, an innocent mistake in the course of a young boy doing what had to be done on a daily basis which I got over and moved on from. However, with the passing of many years, its effect on me personally and on my assumption of what it must have meant to my mother has become magnified. It is enough nowadays with an adult's insight to almost bring me to tears.

I was a young lad, probably ten or eleven at the time it occurred and, whether a reflection of my age or gender or simply my personality, a lot of the tasks I had to perform I felt emotionally detached from. Repetition of tasks reduces their impact, even when the tasks are of a very personal and undignified nature. Dignity is a word that loses its impact after a while when a person has to help another to the toilet day after day. An immunity develops against silly embarrassment.

Around that time, following a visit to the outpatient clinic at Footscray Hospital, Natalia was commenced on indomethacin suppositories. Clearly, these needed to be inserted rectally, one every night, and it was impossible for her to physically insert them herself because of the state of her hands. There was no one else who could perform that task other than me, so every evening when I helped her to bed, she would lay on her left side and I would pull down her pyjama pants and underpants and insert the suppository. This went on for a long time and within a very short time it didn't bother me at all; it just seemed to be another thing that had to be done for the benefit of my mother. I remember the disposable gloves and the gel that the hospital supplied us with and having to unwrap the bullet-shaped suppository from its silver foil wrapper.

I don't know to what extent it bothered my mother. We didn't speak of such things, there was no point. Then, one night, I don't know how it happened, perhaps I had my mind on other things, I put the suppository in the wrong hole. I remember a feeling of awkwardness and apologising to her. I don't really recall what she said other than something to the effect that it was in the wrong spot. More awkward still was having to fish it out again, which seemed at the time to take forever, and replacing it in the correct position and then trying to go on, pulling up her pants, as if nothing had happened.

I think about this incident often. It disturbs me not for my sake but for what it must have been like for my mother. She was a very private, dignified woman and it must have been terribly humiliating for her. I think she coped with it the same way that I did – by blocking it out, by leaving it unspoken and by quickly moving on.

By necessity, a very personal intimacy develops between the carer and the person being cared for that goes way beyond normal human relationships. It is taxing, it is straining and it is devotion. Perhaps love too has a role, in what could arguably be considered its purest form, at least in some cases. As I have stated previously, I think that I loved my mother but even now I'm not sure I understand what I mean by that. She was not an easy person to love and she was not loving, and love, as we generally accept it, requires reciprocation; it will not flourish on a one-way street. Natalia lacked warmth and affection and was far too self-absorbed most of the time to be loveable, and her style of love was very conditional, requiring obedience, loyalty and good behaviour. In my case, unlike my sister's, academic and musical excellence was not a requirement. In that regard, I was spared the torment that she inflicted on her daughter.

Much of Natalia's style of love had to do with her current circumstances of course, but I am sure that the foundations lay in the toughness of her upbringing and a genetic predisposition as indicated by her pre-morbid personality: depressive, pessimistic, demanding. These characteristics taxed Guido to extremes, my sister likewise, and eventually me as well. On her death, I was to feel only relief, not because she no longer suffered but because those who remained no longer did.

20

Trips to the outpatient clinic at Footscray Hospital were a regular and tedious all-day event. Initially, she was taken there by Guido or Adi but once Natalia's condition deteriorated and she was in a wheelchair, she went by ambulance, and once Guido and Adi were no longer available, I went in the ambulance with her. Natalia had never mastered the English language enough to communicate adequately, so I would interpret, wheel her around and get things done, such as taking her scripts to the hospital pharmacy. This necessitated a day off school but my preference would have been to be at school instead of having to attend these mind-numbing, interminable days of much waiting and of watching clock-hands that I'd swear went backwards.

As I mentioned previously, the rheumatology clinic was headed by Dr Mathews MBBS FRACP. Natalia was always happiest when she was seen by him rather than by one of his underlings. His quiet confident style pleased and reassured her. She was also impressed by the letters after his name – FRUCK (as in truck) she called them – and she preferred to be seen by doctors who were FRUCKs. FRUCKs were the only ones she even remotely trusted, the only ones she considered properly skilled and also being seen by a FRUCK reinforced the high opinion she had of herself as an intellectually superior person.

Of course there was very little that even the FRUCKs could do for her at that time other than make a few enquiries, examine her messed-up body and issue a repeat of her anti-inflammatory medications. Often, there were junior doctors or medical students in attendance to learn about her illness, to which she invariably made no objection. To tell her story and to be listened to intently by intelligent young people made her feel special and gave her another opportunity to bask in the warm rays of pity as they gently and kindly examined her deranged joints.

We would more often than not wait around all morning for the ten-minute appointment. Sometimes X-rays would be required before the appointment, more waiting, and finally waiting around at the pharmacy to get the pills. They were days filled with waiting and I dreaded them. I couldn't wait to get back into the ambulance, which was far more interesting to me, for the ride home. For a while, it even made me want to be an ambo but that, as they say, is another story.

Invariably, Natalia would be physically and mentally exhausted after the hospital visits and would go straight to bed. I would be in a state of mental stupor the likes of which only extreme boredom can induce. At any rate, neither of us would be in the mood to cook dinner and I knew, more often than not, what Natalia's preference would be: fish and chips. It was her gastronomic fetish that verged on being an obsession. Sometimes,we had them so often that even I got sick of them or, perhaps more accurately, sick of going to get them. But when she wanted them, she would dig her heels in and could by no means be swayed and would often get quite angry if her demand was refused. So off to the fish and chip shop on Robert Street I'd go, by foot or by bike, and we'd indulge ourselves on those tasty greasy carbs once more.

As well as her regular outpatient appointments, Natalia for a time also attended what was known as the Day Hospital, also at Footscray Hospital. It was one day a week spent doing various activities, craft, physiotherapy and occupational therapy. It was during the school week, so unfortunately it didn't give me much free time to myself but Natalia seemed to enjoy them on the whole. She went through phases, sometimes keen, other times not so, but it was an opportunity for her to get out of the house and to mix with other people, although that was never one of her preferred pastimes, so not surprisingly she mostly kept to herself unless of course there happened to be someone she deemed worthy of spending time with, someone of substance with whom to have serious conversation about world events, politics, family and social issues. According to her, this was a rarity. Few were up to the mark. Most spoke of trivialities or, worst of all, sport.

Some of the things she brought home from the craft sessions made us laugh. There were rag dolls, small tapestries, cushions and ridiculously massive piggy banks made by applying paper-mâché to a balloon, with pieces of cut-out egg carton for the snout and ears. We ended up with about half a dozen of these piggy banks and then we had to start giving them away to reluctant recipients. It was ridiculous. It was like they were breeding despite their lack of sexual organs. They only came in two colours, pink or blue. I assume that boys were blue and pink were girls but who could really tell? There was no other way of telling them apart. It was so funny. Every time Natalia brought another one home, we would roar with laughter. Anyway, there most definitely was never a shortage of repository for loose coins, but sadly, none of them ever came anywhere near to being filled.

Natalia respected the medical profession. In her opinion, the intelligence, education and seriousness of doctors placed them on a higher plane worthy of respect. However,she did not think much of what they had been able to do for her personally, and unfortunately, to be fair, at that time there really wasn't much they could do to curtail aggressive rheumatoid arthritis. So Natalia was both respectful and scornful; a not so surprising paradox in a woman full of paradoxes. She was of course always respectful to their faces and saved the scorn for when she got home. She was almost always like that with other people also, such as friends or relatives we might have visited or who visited us. It would generally be a pleasant enough occasion but she would spend a lot of time afterwards criticising them for their stupidity, commonness, rudeness or greed. It was very difficult for any person on the planet to quite measure up to her ideals of human conduct. Everyone disappointed in one way or another to a greater or lesser extent.

Over a period of fourteen years, Natalia went from walking normally, to walking with a walking stick, then a four-point stick, next a walking frame then finally, in 1974, Michael bought her a wheelchair at a house auction. It was a type with four small wheels that she could propel by shuffling along with her legs and it was easy to transport, so it served her well for many years. Essentially, she could still weight bear enough to transfer herself with assistance, but she never walked more than a few paces again.

It was a terrible thing to witness the progressive capitulation of the body of a woman with a sharp mind who had once been able to create the most wondrous things.

21

Living peacefully with Natalia meant maintaining the house and garden to her satisfaction. It also meant attending to her personal needs. For many years, I was responsible for her medications, her mobility, helping her dress and undress, helping her with toileting, helping her get into and out of bed and chairs and helping her get to appointments. It fell to me to pay bills and manage the finances, which was Natalia's pension and whatever I earned in part-time jobs. I shopped and cooked, washed clothes, ironed, scrubbed and polished floors by hand, cleaned the bathroom, toilet and kitchen, did basic maintenance, did the mowing and worked on the garden. I always had a small vegie patch and would collect horse manure from the nearby paddocks and seedlings from the nearby nursery in Robert Street and we had wonderfully productive peach, nectarine and plum trees yielding rich, sweet and juicy fruit.

As I previously mentioned, I had not been subjected to the intense academic scrutiny which Adi had been forced to endure. I believe that by the time I went through my schooling, Natalia was not so interested in such matters any more. She had her health concerns of course and far less energy to devote to the task of demanding and securing success from her child. It is also my impression that Adi ultimately disappointed her mother by not achieving higher academic glory. Adi had gone on to study music at Melbourne University and was a superb pianist but gave it all away to be a wife and mother. She had committed the most unforgivable sin of underachievement in spite of every opportunity and all of Natalia's work, effort and sacrifice. In my opinion, to Natalia's way of thinking, she would have felt that all her efforts had ultimately been futile so by the time it was my turn, she'd given up on any designs to produce a genius.

I was unaware of what Adi had had to endure at the hands of her mother but I always had a sense that Natalia thought I would never amount to much. I was quiet, kept largely to myself, rarely had an opinion on anything, had zero life experiences and to most people probably didn't seem quite right. But deep down, I quietly determined to show her that I was worthy and that I could achieve something.

Back in the 1970s, it seemed that anyone who did well enough at school either did medicine or law. It was in my fourth year at Footscray High School that, because of my exposure to the hospital environment and a leaning towards science and mathematics, I decided to aim for medicine. When I told Natalia of my decision, she scoffed but her reaction did not surprise me. Her natural pessimism immediately came to the fore, which I took at the time as mum just being mum; of course she was going to consider it impossible. But on later analysis, it occurred to me, and I think I'm right on this, that for her, pessimism was a tool that she used as a guard against disappointment. Sometimes, I find myself doing exactly the same thing when little voices in my head tell me that something is impossible and not to be ridiculous or fanciful; to downplay the expectation of success reduces the level of disappointment if something is not achieved.

She immediately dismissed my idea as a pipe dream, basically saying that it was impossible for a working-class person from the western suburbs to study medicine. Her preference was for me to aim for something far more realistic, such as cooking or tailoring.

Deflating as her reaction was, I didn't let it dissuade me; in fact, it spurred me on. By the time I came to consider my future, Whitlam had opened up tertiary education to everyone. The path was open to all-comers with merit regardless of background. Then I got the marks and Natalia was as ecstatic as I was when the letter of acceptance into the Melbourne University School of Medicine arrived by post.

The letter came in early 1977, a relatively good year. In fact, it was the last relatively good year that Natalia would have.

It was certainly an improvement on 1976. On 8 December of that year, Guido and Natalia were divorced after five years of separation.

Passport photo of Guido, 1977.

Guido was still living in the bungalow at the time. It hurt him greatly when he was served the documents but typically he displayed no anger or violence. He seemed to take it philosophically, as the last of many nails in a very long coffin; merely another blow to be absorbed by his battered mind.

Adi has a copy of the order of the Supreme Court of Victoria given by Mr Justice Anderson. I was placed in the custody of my mother and the question of access by my father was reserved. Guido was ordered to pay $25 per week to Natalia and $20 per week to me, to commence on 15 December 1976. Furthermore, Natalia was granted sole occupancy of the family property (apparently because the continued presence of Guido in the bungalow was an ongoing source of anxiety to her and therefore detrimental to her health). Guido was also required to maintain the property in a reasonable state of repair and to pay $750 towards the cost of Natalia's legal proceedings.

Guido moved to a tiny rental flat in Sunshine, closer to his work. It was all he could afford. It seems a harsh order imposed on a man who had devoted his life to his family, but my mother was ill and unable to work and he was the earner, so he had to pay.

As far as I was concerned, the divorce was a mere formality, a legal dissolution of an entity which had dissolved years earlier. Coming as it did in the wake of my HSC exams, the divorce was completely over-shadowed by other events and had no impact on me whatsoever.

Natalia was pleased. Her legal costs, over which she fretted, were covered and she had a legally binding guarantee of income as well as maintenance of the property. She had won, she had been vindicated, Guido had been kicked out of his own home.

22

In early 1978, Natalia suffered an exacerbation of her rheumatoid arthritis. It required higher doses of prednisolone to achieve remission. Its effect, as always, was rapid and miraculous. Natalia felt better; there was less pain, swelling and stiffness. Understandably, she resisted dosage reductions but the reckoning would come, and it came very suddenly in May of that year.

She was in the kitchen seated in her wheelchair preparing food slowly and as best she could. She reached down to pick up a frying pan and as she lifted it up to the cooktop she sustained a minimal-trauma fracture around the left elbow. It was a trivial everyday action but her osteoporosis had become so severe that the simple act of lifting a small frying pan broke the lower humerus.

The miracle bestowed by the deceitful corticosteroid is not free. One of the costs of the miracle is chalky bones, and there was little in the way of treatment for osteoporosis back then other than supplemental calcium, which of itself is of little benefit unless the diet is lacking in it.

Natalia went back once more to Footscray Hospital. I don't recall if the fracture required reduction, but nevertheless, her arm was plastered and it was clear that she couldn't return home until it was healed.

After the initial treatment, Natalia was transferred to Greenvale Rehabilitation Hospital. A short diary entry some years later recorded her first impressions of the place. She noted, somewhat wistfully one could say, that the hospital was surrounded by green paddocks in which sheep grazed. It was as if the rural setting took her back to Contovello and the Italian countryside. Her fantastical return to Europe was further heightened when she was admitted to the hospital by a Polish doctor. He treated her respectfully and there was a seriousness about him that made her warm to him. They talked about Europe, Poland and her beloved Trieste; her family, and how much she missed them and her homeland. It was good that he made the time to listen to her. This small effort was not forgotten and it was the single point of brightness in her otherwise exceedingly gloomy diary entries.

With the gradual cessation of the prednisolone to allow the fracture to heal, the pain, the joint swelling and the stiffness escalated to such an extent that she could barely move. There followed a long period of institutionalisation: from Greenvale to Mount Royal Geriatric Hospital and finally to a number of nursing homes. None of us could have imagined at that time that it would be almost five years before she returned home.

It was a difficult time for all of us. For Natalia, it represented physical and mental capitulation. Her body was destroyed, she couldn't put any weight on her legs at all and she was completely bedridden for a time. Her skin was pale, smooth and looked feeble, almost artificial, from years spent almost entirely indoors. It was completely unweathered. Lack of activity and long-term treatment with corticosteroids left her tubby, moon-faced, hypertensive and diabetic. Her muscles were devoid of substance, strength and function; they merely lolled about somewhere under the loose skin and fat, barely perceptible, limply doing virtually nothing at all. She had become completely helpless, for a time not even able to feed herself, and certainly way beyond my capacity to help her.

As I mentioned earlier, Natalia kept a diary for a short period of time toward the end of her stays in nursing homes before she returned to her own home in late 1982. It was mostly written in 1981 and 1982, with a few final entries in 1983, and then she gave up on it. Some entries are not contemporaneous; they consist of previous observations and thoughts beginning at the time of her elbow fracture and the initial hospital management. The entries are entirely self-focused and comprise almost exclusively a repetitive litany of woe, despair, self-pity, delusion and paranoia as well as alleged cruelties inflicted on her and her victimisation at the hands of staff and her daughter. Much of it, in my opinion, must be ingested with very large amounts of salt. However, some of the allegations perhaps cannot be entirely dismissed.

I think it is worth recording here some of her writings. They part the curtains and allow us to peer into her state of mind. They describe certain events of alleged cruelty by staff, some of which ring with a tone of truth, although likely to be exaggerated, while others seem fanciful and merely the result of her deep misery, marked introspection, misunderstandings and overwhelming feelings of persecution. For members of the caring professions, whose numbers contain some of the best people humanity has to offer, it is worth reflecting on Natalia's state of mind, and others like her, to perhaps be able to better relate to them.

It was impossible for Natalia to feel contentment. The incidental infliction of pain in the course of her care or therapy was interpreted as deliberate cruelty. Prolongation of pain was seen as calculated torment bordering on torture. Flippant comments, light-heartedness or attempts at humour, well-meant or otherwise, were invariably taken as disrespectful, malicious and sadistic. When treading around Natalia, it was best to say nothing at all other than the most banal courtesies and directions; nothing which could in any way be misconstrued, because she would misconstrue. She required a sympathetic ear and attitude and, above all, a serious and respectful demeanour. To try to lighten her day with jocular comments may have drawn a mild, superficially pleasant response, merely out of politeness, but always went badly deep within her and, given that she was not one to forget or forgive a slight, it would fester and invariably worsen over time as her tortured mind went to work on it.

In one particular nursing home, an old converted house that was never going to be adequate for the purpose of best-practice aged care, there were definite incidents of neglect. The food was poor, the house was dirty and always smelled of stale urine. Musty odours seemed ingrained in everything. Rashes and skin sores went untreated. The residents were showered en masse, each seated on a plastic chair, and hosed down like animals. Natalia complained bitterly, but she always did, so it was often difficult to take her seriously. However, we saw the state of the place and the neglect with our own eyes and smelled the decay with our own noses. The home was completely unsuitable and Adi quickly got her mother out of there.

Around Easter 1981, Natalia writes of another nursing home, bearing in mind that she was only sixty at the time

I am in a nursing home in Melbourne. I have been here for thirteen months. My companion is eighty. Most are over ninety. These poor old people are all mentally unwell and almost all are tied to their seats. I am the only new Australian. In this country the very strong make themselves even stronger, no one wants to spend time or effort on the weak and ill.

On Easter Sunday we had communion. Other people had cards and chocolate. I didn't have any chocolate to give to anyone so I was bullied. This hurt me. The following week was even worse. I felt like a ball being thrown around and they knew I couldn't fight back. My daughter, who is used to big-noting herself, put me in this nursing home because of hate. She enjoys my suffering and isolation. This is my Calvary.

With respect to Adi, in a later entry dated the thirteenth of May 1981, Natalia wrote

What has my daughter got in her conscience to turn so many people against me? When did she start to hate me so much and to desire my death? Why is she so pleased when I suffer and how can she be happy when carnivores laugh at me and torture my rotting body? Why did she try for so long to isolate me from normal people and lock me up in a madhouse with one hundred-year-olds?

In an earlier entry,

One night my whole body was in a lot of pain. The staff asked me what was wrong but I would not tell them because it would have made them very happy and to do everything possible to aggravate my condition.

And on another occasion,

Two staff members helped me to the toilet. I told them my legs were very painful. One said that my legs are all right and that my problem is my relationship with my daughter and that I won't collaborate with them. I tried to explain that my illness has nothing to do with my daughter and that I try to collaborate as much as I can but they wouldn't listen to me.

In an entry dated 28 April 1981, Natalia wrote,

One day one of the nurses told me that she could throw me on the floor and get away with it because no one would believe what I say. I am scared to complain because I would be worse off.

They hate me. All staff have been advised to keep away from me.

They saw me writing and sarcastically asked what I was writing.

Fear and terror are what I feel day and night.

I have been isolated on this continent for twenty-seven years. I have had no good fortune here. I feel very lonely and more and more sad. The suffering scream day and night and for many this is the last spot.

Of the several thousand words that she wrote, there is not one entry that expresses joy, contentment or satisfaction; nor one that can in any way be construed as positive other than the entry already alluded to regarding the pleasant Polish doctor who took his work seriously. It is a record that reflects her introspective gloomy nature as well as her state of mind. That she suffered with depression there can be no doubt and is hardly surprising. She was on antidepressants, but those in use back then were highly likely to cause unpleasant side-effects, adding to her woes. In fact, according to her own records, there seems to be one occasion when she developed urinary retention, which could well have been at least in part medication-related.

To me, reading what she has written for the first time, with the help of my sister, who is much better at translating than me, I am struck by the irrationality of it all and what I consider to be the indecent wallowing in self-pity and martyrdom. Her inability to see good intention in anyone disgusts me and yet, simultaneously, this feeling is tempered by profound sadness and the nagging thought which always comes to me when I am critical of Natalia, which is, in her situation, would I have been any better? I hope I am never in the position to be able to answer that question. It is most unlikely that I ever will be. Would I have conducted myself better or worse when measured against my mother's yardstick? Who can say? For me, it remains the fundamental question whenever I judge her behaviour.

She alleged incidents of cruelty, abuse and neglect that I frankly find hard to believe as a whole, while acknowledging that there may be an element of truth in some of them. Knowing how my mother perceived things, she would have seen the entire process of rehabilitation as wanton cruelty and the infliction of deliberate pain and suffering on the weak by the strong, for no other purpose than their own satisfaction and aggrandisement. She saw the staff as uncaring, ignorant people who did not understand what she was going through. The concept of other people pushing her to become mobile and independent was anathema; she knew her body and mind, and what each was capable of, better than anyone else. Their attempts to force were unnecessary and insulting.

To a large extent, she was right, of course, but she was in a rehabilitation hospital whose aim is to rehabilitate everyone as much as possible, no exceptions, with a view to maximising function and discharge from institutionalised care. Their endeavours may be applauded, they performed their duties as best they could, but in the case of Natalia the broad brush would never work and their efforts were doomed to failure. Natalia's rheumatoid arthritis, now that she was off prednisolone, was out of control and it would seem that this fact was not considered. Her pain was severe, her joints were inflamed, her atrophied muscles were next to useless and her fractured elbow had not yet healed. Rehabilitation at that stage should have been thought of as a process which would take years, not weeks or months, and only possible once her rheumatoid arthritis was better controlled.

Attempts at light-heartedness or banter would have been completely misinterpreted by Natalia and mild or mock rebuke taken very seriously.

In another entry, she states,

> I have been in Greenvale for one week. Two nurses came and got me out of bed. I was completely paralysed. My arms and legs did not move. My legs were dead and the pain was inhuman. While tears fell down my face, I never desired anything as much as to die at that moment. I saw the satisfaction in their faces knowing that I was completely in their hands. They would look at me laughing, the way a cat looks at a mouse. I was so scared. I was praying to die but that wasn't to be.

This reveals clearly Natalia's mental state and the extent of her anguish. While in Greenvale, Natalia had several falls because her legs were so weak. She also lost a lot of weight because she was on a weight-loss diet and off the prednisolone, but also because she didn't like the food and found it very difficult to feed herself, with just her feeble right arm and hand, as she was strenuously, and perhaps excessively, required to do. Adi found the time to go in almost every day to feed her at lunchtime. It was another task performed by a caring daughter that went utterly unappreciated.

> I told my children that I hope death is close. They told me that I have to get out of Greenvale. In my condition you don't win. They were threatening me all the time that I would be punished. The punishment was that I found myself on the floor at least three times a day.
>
> After forty days in Greenvale I went by taxi to Footscray Hospital. My children were there. They removed the plaster from my arm but the fracture had not healed. I did not return to Greenvale. I was admitted to Footscray Hospital where I was treated like a football. Everyone kicked me around and I was called the football of the year. They called me a smelly rat and a skunk and wouldn't even wash my face. I was told I would stay for two weeks in McArthur House and so another Calvary began. I was taking thirty-six tablets a day including twenty for what they call depres-

sion. At night I would dream that I was sleeping on rocks. My dreams are always bad.

One day I went to the Day Hospital. The Indian carer there has saved me from torture so many times. The physiotherapist mocks me and the psychotherapist hates me. This day I was told I would walk out of there. They put callipers on my legs. I cried and fell to the ground. They called me a dirty bitch and kicked me a few times before getting me up again.

This was almost the final entry. There were a couple of short entries; one attacking her sisters for saying that they would come to Australia to visit her but making excuses why they couldn't and the other stating that her daughter refuses to wash her clothes any more (which was true, but only for a brief time because of Natalia's constant ingratitude and antagonism, but my soft-centred sister resumed washing almost immediately).

There was a short letter written to her brother Pepe that was never sent. It was to do with an ongoing dispute within the family because he had taken over the old family home and transferred ownership to himself without any payment to his siblings. Natalia often spoke of this and of the unfairness of it.

Finally, there were two entries in 1983 following the death of Guido, one addressed to me and the other to Adi. To me she wrote,

It is with profound grief that I received the news of the death of your father who was the only man in my life. To you Steven, my sincere condolences, your mother Natalia Reggente Cavini.

To my sister she wrote,

Dear Adi, Michael and grandchildren. The news of the death of your father is very grave even for me. I give you my sincere condolences in particular to you Adi. I know that you loved and looked after him to the very end. Your mother and nonna.

I can't help but find the attempt at sincerity most insincere, knowing full well the misery she inflicted on Guido while he lived. There is of course no love or warmth expressed towards anyone. There is a coldness, a lack of humanity, a total lack of empathy in those short, dutiful statements. They are like the bland press release the Queen might issue in response to a distant tragedy. To me, they are the final insult to a man who had received so many, undeservedly, and all I can say is that I am glad he never read them.

23

While Natalia was in hospitals and nursing homes for four and a half years, I lived alone in the family home, studied medicine and lived largely on takeaways. Alone is not quite right; I shared the home with my pet collie named Cheeky, who loved takeaways every bit as much as I did. I wasted a lot of time. I lived like a slob. I had a couple of close friends from high school with whom I mostly clowned around, played blackjack for small stakes, and that was pretty much it. I didn't have much money, I didn't go out much and there were no girls.

Given the opportunity now presented to me, one could imagine and even expect great parties every Saturday night, but I was a shy kid with few close friends, and I largely failed to connect with my medical student colleagues, who came from another world on the other side of the smog curtain to that which I was accustomed. I was no good with girls. I avoided them as much as possible. They made me nervous and awkward. Their ways were a total mystery to me and I never seemed to have anything to say which could possibly interest them.

I was never a rebellious kid but I wasn't a goody-goody either. Most of the time, I had no idea where to fit in; I seemed to exist in my own personal no-man's-land with only superficial connections to the outer world.

There were only two occasions I can recall where I gave my mother any real teenage-type grief.

The first was the first time I got drunk. I was fourteen and celebrating the end of form three with my best friend Nick from up the street, who was a year older than me. He brought along a full bottle of sweet port. We sat on the bank of Stony Creek, at the back of my place, and got a fire going for the ritual burning of all our school notes from the year just gone. In the coals, we roasted some potatoes in their jackets to have with butter and salt. Once we'd eaten, and with the sun going down, Nick cracked open the port and we sat by the dying fire to enjoy it. I should say that I had never had an alcoholic drink before and I was thoroughly enjoying its oily sweetness. In fact, I was enjoying it so much that within half an hour I had polished off two-thirds of the bottle while Nick, more experienced and perhaps more cunning than I, drank the other third.

The bottle now drained of its luscious contents and the night setting in, we decided it was time to go home. I remember getting about halfway home before collapsing to the ground. Nick got me home somehow and my next recollection is of the anguish on Natalia's face and of her screaming things at me as I waved her away with slurred reassurances on my unsteady way to my bedroom, to sleep the sleep of the dead.

The second time I gave Natalia, and Adi for that matter, real teenage-type grief was even worse, because on that occasion just about everybody got drunk.

It was during form four, around August 1974, that some of the influential-type lads talked about having a party, but not just any party, for the time had come to have one with booze. It was the first time the inner circle had discussed such a radical thing. As a long-serving member of the outer circle, but not entirely without connections that mattered, I saw the opportunity to promote my popularity with those who mattered most. It all seemed very straightforward and my place was ideal, or so I thought. I had a house virtually to myself, with a large garden, with a creek on one side and Grongo on the other, and a mother I could keep in the dark in the lead-up, then keep her tucked safely out of the way in her bedroom, with copious reassurances, during the event. I used my fifteenth birthday as a pretext.

From somewhere, we managed to procure two travel bags full of beer, cask wine and spirits. It was a terrifying amount of grog, which was smuggled in and hidden under the house days before the party.

It began well enough in typical teenage party manner with loud music and a lot of young creatures standing around awkwardly. Natalia was safely ensconced in her bedroom but Adi was there to supervise and to help with the food and soft drinks. Neither were aware that alcohol was present as it was kept outside and if people wanted to imbibe, they had to go outside to do so.

It was all going swimmingly until it became obvious that people were getting drunk. The sordid smell of alcohol was in the air, words became slurred, eyes rolled and went out of focus, people wobbled as they walked, stumbled, fell over, and some of the worst affected were chucking in the lounge room and in the garden. It all went very rapidly downhill from there to become a gigantic, mishmashed fiasco.

Adi tried in vain to restore a measure of decorum but the task was a hopeless one. With hindsight, I feel guilty and very sorry for her. Natalia, sensing with her built-in telemetry that things had gone awry, became irate and bellowed from her bedroom that there was too much noise, she had a headache and for everyone to be sent home.

Just when it seemed things could get no worse, a group of young thugs tried to gatecrash the party and it seemed that people started turning up from all directions. From out of nowhere, the police arrived, but order was slow in being restored. Then, one angry parent after another came to collect their insensible offspring, their darlings who had been reduced to babbling zombies or prostrate blobs wallowing in their own vomit.

The disaster was total. There was no mitigation. The target for their daggers was poor old Adi who, being the sole responsible adult, copped all the flak in what must have been the mother of all attempts of damage control.

It was foolish, reckless and potentially very harmful. Fortunately, no one came to any serious harm but many lost their alcohol virginity that night and no doubt experienced their first hangover the following day. No thought whatsoever was given to possible consequences and the whole episode was totally, utterly, completely irresponsible. Typical teenage stuff really. I look back on it with nostalgic fondness tinged by a little shame. It still makes my sister and me laugh. Natalia wasn't so easily amused. She vowed the next day, as she vigorously and repeatedly made the sign of the cross, that this was the first and last party to be had in her house. Amen. And so it was.

Domestic duties suffered while I lived alone. I'm sorry to say that the house and garden came to look like a slum. Dirty dishes piled up, especially around exam time; then, once the exams were finished, there'd be so many dirty dishes that I had to wash them in the bath. Clothes washing and ironing was neglected, food rotted in the fridge and empty takeaway boxes piled up in the lounge room. The place was dusty and untidy inside; outside wasn't much better. I discovered the tenacity of weeds, and mowing only occurred once the grass was about two feet high or the neighbours politely remarked on the state of the nature strip and the rats and other wildlife living in it. At one point, out of desperation and being thoroughly sick of mowing a jungle with a push-mower that couldn't hack it, I bought a sheep to eat the grass. It was a great hit, so much so that I lent it to my best friend, who was having similar problems with his 'lawns'. Things did not end well for the sheep, however, I'm sorry to say.

Those years alone, away from my mother, saw me reconnect with my father and sister. It was a period of renaissance for me where truth gained a foothold and moments of joy, like golden flowers, basked in the same light that banished the shadows and the dark of the past. There was initially some disquiet. How could there not be? I remained loyal to my mother and the rapprochement with my father and sister came with a sense that I was betraying my mother, but over time those feelings diminished and gradually vanished altogether as I realised they were not the demons I had been led to believe.

Eventually, I spent virtually every Sunday at my sister's home with her and her family and my father. I enjoyed my time with them, I enjoyed playing with my nephew and niece, reading to them, playing cards, kicking the footy and having at least one hearty, healthy meal a week. In short, I enjoyed doing the things that normal families did. It was a revelation.

Natalia was not happy about me seeing them at all, let alone regularly. She knew what it meant, that she was losing her control over me; and she was quite right in that regard but she was no longer in a position to do anything about it.

For some years, I had been a Boy Scout. I enjoyed those years very much. I enjoyed the activity, the bonding, being part of a team, learning new things and collecting badges. It also introduced me to the wonders of the outdoors: nature, camping and bushwalking, and it was the latter that in time would create a firm bond between father, sister and me, as well as a string of unforgettable experiences and memories.

Our first bushwalk together was in January 1979. It was only a two-nighter, but that was sufficient to plant a seed that would germinate and flourish into annual, more extended walks.

We walked the Lerderderg River from O'Brien's Crossing downstream, through the gorge, across the top of Mount Blackwood, then down to the car park at the southern end of the gorge. Despite the heat and the rugged nature of the walk, it was a joyous time together and I was so pleased to have exposed them both to this new experience. I vividly remember deep dark waterholes with precarious tracks at the base of sheer rock faces that we had to tentatively walk along, trying to avoid plunging in. We christened ourselves the Explorers and Guido carved a sign to that effect in wood which Adi still has to this day.

Our second walk was shortly after Christmas 1979. It was longer and tougher but despite that, Guido, now aged sixty, and with minimal preparation, managed the going at his own pace and his truly delightful character shone through, always humorous and never complaining, except as a joke.

This walk was in the high country north of Licola, an area of great beauty which I still revere. We started at the campsite on Breakfast Creek, had breakfast there, and immediately made the tough ascent of Mount Tamboritha, through a lot of trackless terrain. By the end of the day, we had not been able to make the summit due to the steep and scrubby slopes, so we found a suitable place to camp but soon realised that we were surrounded by cows. None of us had any experience of cows and that included how they thought and our collective imaginations quickly launched into fearful images of being charged, stampeded and gored or crushed to death at any moment. Never fear! Guido came to the rescue. As Adi and I relaxed, he scoured the entire mountainside for large, hefty tree branches which he dragged over to fashion a corral of sorts around our tent so we could all have a safe, peaceful and undisturbed night's sleep free from marauding cows with murder in their souls. He really was a wonder and from where exactly he managed to find the energy to do all that remains a total mystery.

The walk continued along an exceedingly picturesque mountain stream called Shaw's Creek, where we spent another night before going across a high plain and then down to the Caledonia River. There we camped, and very quickly another problem presented itself to Guido, for the next morning the river had to be forded. After dinner, while Adi and I relaxed, Guido carted rocks from every corner of the globe to build a crossing which his Lord and Lady could use the next day to keep their dainty feet dry. As a servant, he really was second to none, and all done with his characteristic good humour. It was typical of Guido. If he saw a job that needed doing, he simply got on and did it. There was no idle talk, bitching, moaning or procrastination. He was a doer, not just a talker; and, yet again, exactly what hidden reserves of energy he managed to tap into to be able to lug rocks around for hours remains as mysterious as the dark energy of the universe itself. I suspect its source had something to do with love, his sense of duty and his complete inability to let go of a job he thought needed doing.

The next morning, we successfully crossed the river and managed to stay completely dry, even Adi, whose clumsy attempts to rock-hop were folklore and always a great source of entertainment. There followed another very steep climb on a rudimentary track to the summit of the Crinoline. By now, Guido and Adi had well and truly developed a severe phobia of contour lines that were close together on the map. They went into a panic attack whenever brown was the dominant colour on the way ahead. They had also begun to question my leadership, doubting me when I proclaimed that the terrain was merely undulating. They also complained like lower-class rabble with a persecution complex that I always chose the most difficult route. My attempts to explain that there was no other way invariably fell on deaf ears. There was much amusement at my expense and a lot of laughs.

Adding to our woes was the not insignificant matter of running out of food, so lunch that day consisted of taking it in turns to scoop from the jar with our fingers what remained of the Vegemite! Fear not, however, for all ended well. As the day drew to a close, and after a punishingly steep descent of the Crinoline, we reached Breakfast Creek, where Michael had a barbecue going. To this day, I remember the smell of cooking meat and onions as it drifted up to us. We'd spent most of the day talking about it. It was all our hungry minds wanted to talk about and it did not disappoint. It was a meal I shall never forget.

Our third walk was shortly after Christmas 1980. It was tougher again, and yet again, full of priceless memories. It is, in my opinion, the best inland walk in Victoria; the country around the Terrible Hollow, at the headwaters of the Wonnangatta River.

We commenced this walk on the Wonnangatta River downstream of the Moroka with Adi's children, Jason and Natalie, with us for the initial easier part of the walk. It was delightful walking, simply following the Wonnangatta upstream, some sections entirely trackless. The first night, we camped on an island at the confluence with the Moroka and the second night we camped at the site of the old Wonnangatta homestead where we came upon a suburbia of other campers with all the camping mod cons and generators blaring. The final day with the kids was a long ascent up to Howitt Plains, which they managed without too much complaint.

I remember camping that night on the plain with the evening waning and the crisp cool air crawling through us as the light faded. To the west, there was still some orange-yellow glow from the set sun which highlighted a crescent moon and a couple of stars against the deep gun-barrel-blue sky elsewhere. It was a stunning sight which became deeply embedded in my psyche. For me, it is a paradigm of the ideal sunset, seen from a lonely and isolated plain, and I think of it whenever I see one similar, but never one better.

The next day, we left the kids with Michael and descended back to the Wonnangatta River via a different and seemingly interminable route which saw us emerge further upstream from where we had been before and it was there that we camped.

It was an ongoing joke on all our walks that Guido would take about an hour every night to get himself organised and settled before he could finally relax and get to sleep. He fluffed around getting his gear organised, his bedding organised. Next, he had to find somewhere secure to hang his glasses, and then find an escape-proof spot for his dentures, as he was convinced that they strolled around during the night because, so he claimed, the following morning they were never to be found where he had left them. With the rigmarole finally completed, he put his head down on his makeshift pillow only to find within a matter of minutes that a family of crickets were merrily chirping directly under his earhole. As one can easily imagine, this rather pissed him off. Clearly this would not do and very soon a distressing situation for him became a most distressing situation for all of us as, once again, it took him an hour to rearrange everything before we could all finally get some sleep. Adi and I laughed so much it brought us to tears. It still makes us laugh, but the tears are a little different now.

Needless to say, the next morning we were all a little under par. But the show had to go on. From there, the walk took us through trackless terrain up and along the Blue Hills before steeply striking up to the twin horns of the Viking. We spent a long time on the summit of the first horn taking in the extraordinary and uninterrupted view south to the Wonnangatta valley. It was a difficult view to part with.

As the day was getting on and we were pretty exhausted from the climb, we decided to camp in the saddle between the two horns.

We kept the following day easy and merely pushed on to Viking Saddle, a pretty spot of lower ground between the Viking and the Razor, to camp. The rest was a blessing as the next day was hot and tough going. The Razor, with its long chain of baking summer rocks and scrubby tracks, was a difficult summit to reach, but fortunately the rest of the day across Mount Despair and then on to Catherine Saddle was much easier. The grassy flats of the saddle, with water nearby, was a perfect place to camp, if you discount the terrifying thunderstorm that came through that night.

Having survived Armageddon, the following morning saw us ascend Mount Speculation, an incomparable summit and a sublime vantage point from which to experience the surrounding mountains and the astonishing view deep down into the Terrible Hollow itself. It was a moment Adi and I still treasure and it filled Guido with wonder, so much so that it became his favourite mountain, and so, many years later, Adi and I returned to the same spot to scatter some of his ashes.

We almost froze to death camping on the summit of Mount Buggery, experienced the majesty of traversing the Crosscut Saw and scaled Mount Howitt before returning to Macalister Springs. The walk was not easy, especially for poor old Guido, but he kept going, pacing himself as he would say, and it was truly wonderful.

Our fourth and unfortunately final walk together was shortly after Christmas 1981. This was the magnificent Overland Track in Tasmania from Cradle Mountain to Lake St Clair. It was once again full of amazing experiences and memories. We took our time – seven nights out – we didn't want to rush through this magnificent countryside. As it was, we lost a full day due to heavy rain so the extra time available was a boon.

My nephew Jason made up a foursome. He was eight years old at the time and did very well. Guido, however, did not go so well. It was the first time that he felt chest pains and he would get short of breath far more easily. He also lacked his usual vigour and clearly struggled despite using the Ventolin inhaler he had brought along.

I recall such wonders as Mount Pelion West and scrambling to the rocky summit of Mount Ossa, Tasmania's highest, and have since learnt of their names being connected with Greek mythology. The terrain was indeed stunning, but it was all tempered by the ominous failing of Guido's health.

In 1982, Guido saw a respiratory physician at the Royal Melbourne Hospital, Dr Michael Pain, and after tests were performed, he was diagnosed with adenocarcinoma of the lung, which had spread, as numerous small nodules, throughout both lungs, into the pleura and the pericardium. It was inoperable and incurable, beyond any treatment available at that time. The only option was palliation. He was sixty-three years old and very much looking forward to retirement after a life of hard work. This was to be denied him. It was not deserved, it was not undeserved, it was simply life playing out as it does.

Guido accepted the ebbs and flows of life as he accepted most things. Any bitterness, anger or sense of unfairness he kept to himself. He never whined. One of Guido's dreams was to have a small house in the country somewhere, anywhere really, just somewhere he could go to relax, tinker, do a bit of fishing and get away from everything. So to that end, in late 1982, we bought an old miner's cottage in a remote town in the middle of nowhere called Gaffney's Creek. Guido put in most of the money, Adi and I put in the rest, and we still own it to this day. Guido went there only twice before he died but the walls are adorned by a lot of his artwork. It is a wonderful place of escape and tranquillity and it is also where the other half of his ashes are scattered; the rest, as previously mentioned, are on his favourite mountain, Mount Speculation. There is a small and simple bronze plaque at the cottage where his ashes were placed. It gives the date and place of his birth and the date and place of his death; they seem so far apart. It also states that he was a dear and beloved father and nonno.

In late 1982, I did my final year medical exams. Guido was there to help me. He did what cooking and cleaning he could, which wasn't a lot by that time because of his poor health, but he was there, in his usual unobtrusive way. As instructed, he made sure that I woke early on the morning of an exam so I could get in a final cram. He did not tell me at that time that he was dying of cancer, because he did not want it to distract me from my studies. My understanding at that time was that he merely had bronchitis and asthma as a result of a long history of intermittent smoking and his exposure to toxic smoke at his place of work but, notwithstanding the intensely single-minded state I was in at the time, I vividly recall an evening when he came into my room to say goodnight and his appearance shook me like a slap on the face. He looked drained, thin, a little short of breath, and his body leaned to one side because of the pain in his chest.

As he turned and feebly shuffled away, the realisation came to me that he was dying. It had penetrated the hard shell of my self-interest, which is so crucial at exam time, and struck something soft within me that I didn't know existed. I'd seen enough of people dying even as a final year medical student to grasp that there could be no doubt and no hope for him and yet here he was sacrificing himself for me in this way. I didn't let on that I knew; I immediately understood the reason behind the secrecy, the conspiracy of silence, but once he'd gone back to his own bed, I cried. I was hard, it took a lot to make me cry, but on that night I cried a lot and it was serious crying, the sort that wrenches the gut and gushes forth from a very deep pain and sadness.

I wasn't told about Guido's illness until after my final exam. Guido, Adi and myself sat together. It was a solemn occasion. I was given all the details that thus far had been kept from me.

Guido died on 13 June 1983 in the Royal Melbourne Hospital, where he had spent only his last few days. Adi had done an incredible job caring for him in her home until then. In the final days, in a state of terminal disease and drug-induced delirium, it was his beloved Lina that he called out to; the Lina he cherished; the Lina I'd never known.

In accordance with his wishes, we had a simple, secular service at Altona Crematorium. There was a small gathering. He didn't have a lot of friends, only a few close ones. It was family that mattered most to him.

24

Before Christmas 1982, Natalia was finally well enough to return home from the nursing home. It was prompted by the imminent visit of her sister Aniça from Italy. Once home, she immediately tried to impose the old order but I resisted; those days were gone. I was twenty-three years old and a medical graduate; things had changed.

Again, she attempted to turn me against my father and sister but in so doing she unwittingly succeeded only in turning me against her. Again, she was desirous of me being her personal servant, but now I stood my ground and rebelled against her. I was willing to help with her personal care if needed but I insisted that she do as much as she could herself, and I certainly wasn't getting down on hands and knees to scrub floors any more.

Aniça arrived with her husband Marcello (known as Cello), to visit Natalia but also to see Guido for the last time. They stayed for one month and both were an absolute delight. They weren't your average tourists, they weren't interested in seeing Australia, they had come to see us.

In typical Italian nonna style, Aniça thought I was far too thin so while they were staying with us, she cooked me three meals a day, large meals, irresistibly delicious home-cooked Italian meals, as only nonnas are capable of producing. Also, in common with all nonnas anywhere in the world, she totally disregarded any appeals for dietary restraint. Words or phrases such as no, no more, I'm full, I've had enough, I really can't fit any more in, I'll explode, simply did not register with Aniça; in fact, they were disdainfully swept aside as her chubby arms dished up more food onto your plate. With no trouble at all, in fact, with the greatest pleasure, I managed to put on six kilograms in one month! This achievement pleased Aniça, it was a job well done, but it made me feel like a satisfied slob. The diet began the day she left.

When Aniça wasn't cooking, she was going to the Queen Victoria Market or the local Italian grocer. That's all she wanted to do!

Cello was much the same in the sense that he didn't want to go anywhere either. He was happy just to hang around with us and do jobs around the place. He smoked a lot, perhaps drank a bit too much at times, and remarkably, despite having Aniça fuss over him for so many years, he managed to remain skinny as a rake. He had an extraordinary capacity to say no to her and thus conquer her insatiable appetite to fatten people up. He was the only one she accepted no from without argument; an understanding reached after so many years spent with an indomitable partisan.

While here, he kept himself busy and built Adi a superb brick barbecue on the Maribyrnong River flats at the back of her property in Ascot Vale; it still stands. He was a restless soul who liked to keep active, was highly prone to boredom and was thus, with a very keen eye, incessantly on the prowl for tasks.

I was most impressed by how much they seemed to genuinely care for each other and give each other the freedom to simply be themselves. In them, I saw for the first time a blueprint for marriage; that in spite of their differences of temperament, perhaps marriage could work through sufficient application of tolerance and mutual respect.

One day, I had the temerity to take them to see a small part of this wonderful country. They resisted but I insisted. It was an argument which, as their host, I was compelled to win, albeit with a large measure of tenacity. I don't know what I was thinking, as it was pretty much a total failure from the start, but I was determined that they see something, anything, at least once during their stay, other than Footscray, Ascot Vale and Queen Victoria Market.

I took the intrepid decision to take them to our cottage at Gaffney's Creek in Guido's rickety brown Cortina. The car felt like we wouldn't make it out of Melbourne but she managed the four-hour drive to get there, the last hour on rough dirt road, what's more. Crossing the Goulburn River must have seemed like crossing the Styx to this couple of stay-at-home Italians and as the isolation grew so too did their trepidation.

I had intended to stay the night, but after a couple of hours at the cottage poking around, I sensed that, despite some politeness on their part, whatever enthusiasm they'd mustered had well and truly waned. It was all far too remote and wild and rustic, there were no shops, and the cooking facilities weren't up to scratch at all. Explorers they were not. They were most keen to get back to civilisation and I tried not to let my disappointment show.

We took a different route home; more bone-rattling dirt roads through Woods Point and Marysville that seemed to go on forever. The sense of isolation increased as the sun set and the gloom of evening emerged. With the darkness, and sensing their growing anxiety, a feeling of foreboding came over me, then, just before Healesville, and with a certain justifiable sense of inevitability, the car broke down. It was as if the circumstances and our collective trepidation had willed it so.

By now, it was completely dark and the legendary Italian dramatic panic was welling in Aniça. Cello and I managed to keep her relatively calm and I reassured her as much as humanly possible that the RACV would not let us perish, that they would save us, which they duly did; thus peace was restored.

It was an exceedingly long day with about eight hours of driving but we made it home from the wilds of Victoria in one piece. Cello and Aniça were most relieved and, not surprisingly, not too keen on any more expeditions into the Australian never-never.

At that time, Guido was too unwell to live alone. He lived at Adi's house with her family. Shortly after his diagnosis was confirmed, Adi told Natalia the news and her reaction was minimal and dismissive. In fact, because Guido was no longer able to work, she thought it was a ploy on their part to stop Guido's maintenance payments to her. She instructed her solicitor of the situation, who in turn sought medical confirmation and only then was she convinced of the veracity and seriousness of his illness. Her capacity to trust her own daughter on even the gravest matter was non-existent and her callous attitude angered me.

After Cello and Aniça had been in Australia for a couple of weeks, staying mostly with Natalia and me, an incident occurred which was most distressing and consequential. It was a mid-afternoon and I can still recall the warm sunlight coming through the square west-facing windows of the small kitchen-dining area. Aniça, as usual, was cooking. She had prepared a watery broth that I detested called *brodo*. Several times as a kid I'd had my face dunked in it because I wouldn't eat it and on one occasion I even ran away from home because of *brodo*, only to return a few hours later with the approach of darkness and with my tail well and truly between my legs. *Brodo* and I already had some history of which this event was to be the latest and most sinister chapter.

Cello and I sat at the small dining table talking. He smoked and we watched Aniça go about her business. They were about to go to Adi's house and Aniça was ladling some of the *brodo* into a container to take to Guido when Natalia entered the room on her motorised wheelchair. I knew straight away that she was in a mood and ready for a fight and I also knew why.

'What are you doing, Aniça?' she demanded, with a tone of unrepressed annoyance.

But on this occasion Natalia faced a formidable opponent, one not easily intimidated. Aniça was not a shrinking violet or a shrinking anything else for that matter. I could see raised hackles on both sides of the ring and then the bell rang for the bout to begin.

'We are going to see Guido and Adi. As you can well see, Dali, I've made *brodo*, and I'm taking some for Guido,' she replied, in a cuttingly reasonable tone.

'No!' Natalia immediately shrieked. 'This is my kitchen, this is my home, and that is my meat that I paid for. I don't want this sort of thing going on in my home. I won't allow it!'

'Yes, it is your home and we are your guests but I want to take some *brodo* to a sick man who is dying of cancer and you can't stop me from doing that. We are Christians and it is a Christian thing to do.'

'I don't care about Christians or non-Christians. Christ has abandoned me just as much as my family has abandoned me. I am here suffering alone and so should he.'

Cello and I tried to intervene but reason had left the room and was by now well on its way up Stony Creek somewhere. We were not heard and remained mere observers of an increasingly volatile catfight.

'You are so full of hate, Dali, that you make no sense. I bought this meat, I bought these vegetables, because I knew that you wouldn't like it if I used yours. This *brodo* comes with me. I'm not interested in whether you allow it or not.'

'Yes Aniça, this is the first time you have spoken the truth. I am full of hate because everyone has hated me. And now I'm even betrayed by my own sister. You should be ashamed. Take the *brodo*, if it means so much to you, and go, but don't ever come back! Never!'

The three of us, Aniça, Cello and I, were stunned. I felt embarrassed and very angry. I decided to go with them and we took the *brodo* and left immediately, leaving Natalia to steam in her own toxic juices and perhaps even contemplate and feel some remorse for what she had just said but I knew that was unlikely just as I knew an apology would never pass her lips.

Following the argument, Cello and Aniça stayed at Adi's house for the remainder of their time in Australia. Other than an awkward goodbye when they left to return to Italy, it was the last time they would see Natalia.

In the wake of Natalia's argument with her sister, my own anger towards her would not subside. It got worse. I could no longer stand being with her; she disgusted me. I was tired of her self-pity, her petty nastiness and her incessant attempts to manipulate others. I now realised that it wasn't just Guido and Adi, and perhaps even me now, that she hated and could not get along with; she hated everyone and could not get along with anyone because she blamed everyone for her demise and envied everyone who could still find some joy in their lives. Everything was so unfair to her.

That incident was the final straw for me. I had come to hate my mother. I left home a short time later to live with a friend during my intern year. I left her to her own devices, to sink or swim alone. I didn't care about her or whether she managed or not any more. I refused to see her for eighteen months and I hoped that she would learn something from it but I don't think she ever did.

25

My sister was more forgiving and more duty-bound towards Natalia than I was. She continued to wash Natalia's clothes and visited her once a week at Waratah Street; and was despised for doing so.

Natalia often asked after me but I stubbornly refused to yield to her requests that I visit her. I felt that she had forfeited the right to any kindness and needed to be punished for her behaviour, and I chose my absence as the means of achieving this. I feel sure she would have interpreted it as yet another unfairness inflicted on her by her cruel family, but for me, I simply needed some time away from her and to ever live with her again was completely out of the question.

When Adi's marriage broke down in 1984, Adi alleged that she had been assaulted by her husband and continued to live in fear of further violence. She desperately wanted herself and her children to be safe. The family home in Ascot Vale was sold and she bought a smaller home in West Essendon with her share of the proceeds. However, there was an eight-week period between moving out of the former and moving into the latter. She asked Natalia if she and the two children could live with her for that period of time; the request was refused on the basis that Natalia was afraid that Michael would try to break into the house. I was appalled at the time that a mother could so callously refuse a desperate request from her daughter, but with the benefit of hindsight, it was the correct decision. Adi and her children needed somewhere safe where they could not be found and sure enough, on one occasion, Michael did call on Natalia seeking Adi's whereabouts. Who knows what might have happened if he'd found her there?

I had recently bought a house in Yarraville with my girlfriend, but it was being renovated at the time, so we couldn't accommodate them.

In the end, they spent the eight weeks in a caravan park in Brooklyn until they could finally find refuge in their new home. They lived in a caravan for that time; the accommodation was rough and cramped and a lot of the language and style of their neighbours was rough as well, but the location was secret and they were safe.

Natalia managed to live at home alone for almost four years, which was a remarkable feat and a testament to her burning desire for solitude and independence in her own home, for which she was willing to pay any price. She used a motorised wheelchair and was able to transfer independently. She had full community services consisting of regular home help, district nursing and meals-on-wheels. As with virtually any older Italian you'd care to speak to, the meals-on-wheels was not a hit. Adi visited once a week with her children, did some cooking of meals of a more palatable nature for her and washed her more delicate items of clothing. As usual, it was the children who brought Natalia some cheer. Jason and Natalie, I believe, genuinely liked their nonna and felt sorry for her and tried to make her happy when they visited. These were the only occasions when Natalia's woes were temporarily displaced by a little joy.

This period of relative calm and the final bastion of independence came to a sudden and inevitable conclusion one day in 1986 when Natalia had a fall getting into bed. Her right femur disintegrated. She was taken by ambulance to the emergency department at what was then known as the Western General Hospital in Footscray (the former Footscray and District Hospital). In 1986, I was an emergency registrar at that very hospital and I was on duty the day she arrived but I left it to one of the other doctors to treat her. Once the extent of her injury became known, it was clear that her right femur was shattered into dozens of pieces because of the extreme severity of her osteoporosis. Surgical treatment was out of the question; there was literally nothing left of the bone that could in any way be operated on. She was transferred to the orthopaedic ward, which at that time was adjacent to her old haunt, Macarthur House. Her right leg was placed in traction, she was given analgesia, and other than general nursing care, there was little else that could be done. Clearly, her hospital stay would be a long one and the prospect of her femur somehow healing sufficiently for her to return home was virtually an impossibility.

The development of pressure sores was inevitable in someone bed-ridden, in traction and where movement was difficult and very painful. It was an unimaginably trying time for Natalia. Then, after some weeks of traction that produced no sign of healing of the femur at all, came another blow: Natalia's right thigh turned into a huge abscess. The choice became suddenly stark: amputation of the right leg or death. I recall discussing this matter with my mother. True to past form, her initial reaction was to vehemently choose death as her sole release from further suffering, but I didn't believe her. She had so often in the past talked about wanting to die that I couldn't take it seriously now, even though the loss of a leg meant a permanent loss of independence. Perhaps callously, I came to interpret her wishes to die more as calls for pity rather than reflecting a serious intent to perish. Therefore, I was not surprised when she eventually consented to have the amputation.

Fundamentally, despite multiple morbidities, she had a very tough constitution. She survived the operation, then followed a long period of recovery once again back in Macarthur House, the geriatric ward known unflatteringly as Mac Shack. Intravenous was followed by oral antibiotics and her small stump healed surprisingly well and quickly. After another period of rehabilitation during which nothing of a particularly useful nature could be rehabilitated, Natalia was ready for discharge. A return home was impossible. Natalia would spend the rest of her days in nursing homes.

Natalia spent some years at Villa Franca, a nursing home in Werribee that specifically cared for people of Italian background. She was reasonably happy there, though she complained bitterly a lot of the time depending on her mood, her level of pain or her interpretation of the behaviour of people around her. At least there were a lot of other Italians there, some of whom she could communicate with, but at the age of sixty-six, she was still very young to be in such a place where most people were in their eighties or nineties and often not of sound mind.

Despite the drive, Adi or I visited her quite regularly. Sometimes, she was glad to see us; at other times, when she wasn't so glad and immediately gave us grief, we would promptly turn around and leave. We quite often brought her home, either to my place or Adi's, for a day or two, and always at Christmas, Easter, Mother's Day and for her birthday. She was never abandoned by her family in spite of her regular claims to the contrary.

It was at Villa Franca that I introduced Natalia to my latest girlfriend, then fiancée, then wife, Gena. Our wedding was in Bairnsdale in 1990, which Natalia had been unable to attend. It was also at Villa Franca where Natalia was introduced to my first child, Simon, born on 13 September 1991. She was not destined to meet my second child, Jessica, born in 1993. As happened in the past with Adi's children, it was only the presence of young life, sweet and blameless, that seemed to bring her any genuine joy and a truly warm smile to her face.

After several years at Villa Franca, we were able to transfer Natalia to a nursing home in Ascot Vale called Marivale so she could be closer to us. Of all the nursing homes she had been to, she seemed happiest at Marivale. It was a modern, clean, bright and purpose-built facility and, from our point of view, the staff were excellent, but from Natalia's point of view, any contentment, I think, merely reflected the fact that we were close by and could visit more frequently, even if it was just a quick pop-in to drop something off.

At this time, after so many years of struggle and now aged seventy, her general health was deteriorating. She had diabetes, high blood pressure, her heart was beginning to fail and her immune system was less robust. She became more prone to infections, particularly respiratory and urinary, and it was the latter which would snatch her life.

Natalia had always been superstitious. Spiders in the house were meant to bring money. If her right eye twitched, something good would happen; if her left, something bad. She was also suspicious about Easter. It was her firm belief that only bad things happened around this time. In the week before Easter 1992, she suddenly became very ill. She'd had another urinary infection, but this time the infection spread to her bloodstream. She developed what is a very serious complication known as gram negative septicaemia, which resulted in the rapid onset of shock and unconsciousness, from which she never recovered.

Natalia spent her last few days in the Royal Melbourne Hospital before my sister and I made the decision, guided by her treating doctors, to cease all active treatment. For me, it was a relatively straightforward decision. I saw that she had suffered enough, I saw that her children had endured enough, I saw the wreckage that her body had become, and I saw no prospect at all of her having a future life worth living, even if that was at all possible. I saw all these things very clearly at that time but what I felt most of all was relief, and what I wanted most of all was for everything to be finally over.

For Adi, the decision was more difficult and it took some persuasion to finally convince her of the futility of continuing with treatment. I admired yet disagreed with her thinking. Adi, even in these final moments, was not yet willing to give up on her mother despite the incalculable reams of psychological wreckage her mother had left her with.

For me, the decision was black and white and based on scientific reasoning; for Adi, it went to questions of faith itself. She thought in greys and what-ifs. What if Natalia could get well again? What if a miracle could happen and did happen? Can a person be denied the chance of a miracle? Natalia's final decline had been sudden and left Adi unprepared for the finality of her death. She sought hope, any hope, in a hopeless situation. In spite of all that she had endured from her mother, Natalia was her mother and Adi was unwilling for a time to accept her death and to allow herself to commit the final act of betrayal – give her consent to the cessation of treatment.

In the end, the decision was made. Active treatment was ceased. Nature or God, depending on your views, was the final arbiter. A priest attended for the final sacrament. Natalia never regained consciousness and died on 16 April 1992, Maundy Thursday, a time at which she believed something bad always happened. Adi and her son Jason were there at the time of her final breath and heartbeat; I was working.

There is one other thing I should mention at this point and I'm not exactly sure why I did it. It was nothing morbid. I think that at the time I just wanted to do some final act to remember my mother by – take one final look into her imponderable soul. It was the last time I saw Natalia alive; she was unconscious and hadn't spoken for days. There was no way to communicate with her but I desperately wanted a last act of communication with my mother before she was gone forever and I also wondered if somewhere deep inside she was aware of what was going on. As her condition deteriorated, this thought recurred and nagged me: how could I get through to her one last time and how much awareness was left? So, shortly before her death, as we stayed at her bedside, I leant over her and opened her left eye. For some moments, it blankly stared back at me but then I felt as if she could see me and what I saw in that eye was fear.

Thinking back now to that time, I am not proud of my role in the decision to stop her treatment nor in swaying my sister to reach the same conclusion. I strongly believed then and still do that medically and ethically it was the correct decision and I used the full weight of my medical background to convince Adi of the facts of the matter as well as to ease her pained conscience. But I'm afraid to say that my motives were largely selfish and no amount of scientific reasoning can change that fact. The simple, human fact is that Adi wanted her mother to live and I wanted her to die. I no longer thought of Natalia as a mother. I did not love her; to me, she was simply a burden that I had had enough of. I felt it was time to put an end to her miserable existence and to the misery she inflicted on others. The truth was that I simply wanted her gone.

These thoughts did not pain my conscience at all at the time because my concealed motives were immaterial to the justification for stopping treatment. It was not until later in my life that some pangs emerged. They are still there, and show no sign of going away.

Human emotions are complex, deeply involved, ground out over a lifetime, and they can be glossed over by rational thought and action, but they do not go away simply by acts of will.

It was 1998 before Natalia's ashes were taken to Contovello by her cousin Nini, who also lived in Melbourne. She had finally returned home, back to the place she had never wanted to leave, to her mother's bosom.

26

So, dare I add my name to the endless list of those who have asked what meaning is to be found in life; and, more specifically to me, Natalia's life? It is surely a question which has vexed humanity since we developed the capacity to think and to no longer be mere slaves of instinct. At some point in our past, we progressed from thinking, I'm hungry, I must eat; or I'm horny, I must have sex. We moved beyond what had largely been the sole concern of animals and began to torment ourselves with higher abstract thinking and ideas.

In my opinion, such philosophical concepts have certainly managed most admirably to fill bookshelves, and may even have made for interesting, thought-provoking reading, but fundamentally they have achieved little else. To me, for all our complex thinking, we have scarcely progressed at all from what matters to lesser thinking animals and any pretence of a deeper philosophical understanding of life's meaning is false and merely the opinion of one person who assumes to have discovered the answers to their own subset of riddles and therefore to know what is best for others. There are countless examples in history of people who have arrogantly thought they knew what was best for everyone else and imposed their will in one way or another, virtually always with disastrous consequences.

The notion of a meaning of life is as varied as people are varied and can only be answered in vague ways which may apply to some people but not all. I believe in individualism. Each must find their own meaning, whatever that may be, if that is what matters to them, without trying to impose on others; or you can simply take life as it comes, as Guido did, without all the worry about meanings and the trials to fulfil them.

I very much doubt that lesser animals concern themselves with finding meaning in life. Their concerns are much more straightforward: individual survival and survival of the species. It is humans who are burdened by the desire, the expectation, for more: to achieve, to be a force for change, to leave a mark and to have somehow made a difference in whatever way possible with the tools given us. This sets us apart from merely being born, existing for a short period of time, maybe reproducing and certainly dying. And yet, for the vast majority of people, this is precisely their lot. Very few leave a permanent mark, fewer still are remembered beyond a couple of generations, the rare few are immortalised. It is these unfulfilled expectations which, I believe, are the root of much human unhappiness. Most of us live for no enduring purpose whatsoever other than replacing ourselves with our offspring, and we have trouble accepting that. Because we can think, we think that there must be more, but there really isn't. We exist for a time, and then we no longer exist. If you can find some deeper meaning to that, which helps you in some way, then good for you, I respect it, but I reject any broader value.

And what of Natalia's life? What meaning, if any, can be gleaned from it? Much has been spoken and written of the constructive and destructive nature of suffering. It is perhaps the most fundamental paradox. In my life, firstly as a carer for my mother, then as a medical practitioner, I have seen a lot of suffering and I feel qualified to make some observations on it.

A distinction must be made between short-term and long-term suffering. Short-term suffering can be constructive, virtuous and ennobling. Its stoic resistance can inspire others; no better example can be found than that of the final days of Jesus. It has the power to force us to refocus and re-prioritise like nothing else. It can be a most wondrous tool for not only learning about ourselves and improving ourselves, but also for shining a bright light on those around us, to indicate those we should esteem and those we shouldn't. And as a human collective, it is a binding agent, a conduit from selfish to selfless, with an extraordinary capacity to bring about surprise in the actions of oneself and others; good and bad.

However, to my way of thinking, for suffering to be in any way positive, it must have an ending or at least the hope of one. There must be a light, real or perceived, at the end of the tunnel. Beyond a certain indefinable point, the longer suffering must be endured, the more destructive to the individual or the group it becomes. There is no value whatsoever in remorseless, lifelong suffering with no prospect of relief. Such suffering, when there is no hope of succour, is entirely destructive to the mind, body and soul.

Total destruction was Natalia's most unfortunate lot. There is no better word than destruction to describe her life; and of course what went with it was the partial destruction of those locked in orbit around her.

Destruction set me on the road to atheism. I mean no disrespect to those who have faith, for they are as entitled to their beliefs as I am to mine, but I have never experienced any evidence of a benevolent God. It is my personal observation that God is either non-existent or completely indifferent and I prefer to believe the former rather than the latter, for the latter makes no sense at all.

If we truly were to be condemned to an eternal recurrence of the same, then Natalia would find herself existing in hell right here on Earth. I believe there is not one aspect of her life that she would consider heavenly nor wish to relive, including that of becoming a mother, for she had spent the greater part of her childhood being a mother already, so that by the time she had children of her own, they were more inconvenience than joy. She would by that time, I'm sure, have preferred to devote the requisite time and energy to her own life and career.

Natalia's marriage to Guido was a mistake. I'm sure that the courtship was fun and the fun would have lasted for a while into the marriage but I fear that their decision to marry was made in haste and under the shadow of war. They were incompatible. Perhaps Natalia and the cellist would have been better suited. They might have had a wonderful life together, perhaps remained childless and been thoroughly happy excelling in their own careers but who's to know – life does not come with a rewind button.

It is also my belief that Natalia should not have had children. She had only the briefest life of her own before Adi was born, and at a deeper level she completely lacked the warmth and selflessness needed to be a good parent. To her daughter, she was cold and cruel. She sought to use her as a tool for the vicarious achievement of those things which had been denied her, but I have no doubt that in Natalia's eyes her daughter mostly disappointed. Towards me, there was some warmth at times. Perhaps I was seen as innocent of all that had gone on before. I was never blamed or hated as much as my sister was, although there always existed the undertone of blame that my birth had brought on her rheumatoid arthritis. I think too that mothers are more forgiving of their sons, just as fathers are more forgiving of their daughters. But on a more pragmatic level, Natalia needed me; she had no one else. Furthermore, I feel that she had no particular expectations of me, so I didn't disappoint.

Natalia's was an unfortunate life. It was pathetic. Her suffering was meaningless, her life was meaningless, her suffering was her life. Suffering fuelled her insatiable furnace of self-pity. Nothing pleased her more than the pity of others; the pity we all feel for the undeserving victim. It was all she had and it placed her above others. The suffering she had to endure made her righteous, superior and entitled but her misery turned people away. It was always there and they tired of it. It stared them in the face and it was her entire focus and it created a barrier between her and the rest of humanity. She had very little else to talk about.

Suffering was her crowning achievement. I'm sure she felt that she had suffered more than virtually any other human in history. Positives were whitewashed as they detracted from her status as a supreme sufferer and she actively perpetrated the myth of her abandonment by the family to further enhance the perception, in her own mind as well as in the eyes of others, of her enormous suffering.

Perhaps I am being too cruel, but particularly once her mental state deteriorated after 1978, there was nothing more to her life. Her depression, delusion, paranoia, suspicion and superstition made it so.

The relief I felt with Natalia's passing lasted a long time. Everything to do with her had finally ended but the hatred is now long gone; a thing of the past. Nowadays, I am more inclined to feel deeply sorry for her; for her physical suffering of course, but more for the mental torment of an intensely dissatisfied life, devoid of anything that could in any way be described as meaning, where nothing went according to plan.

We have very few photos of Natalia from the last ten years of her life. She detested having her photo taken because of her appearance. The final photo we have of her was taken in September 1991, when she was introduced for the first time to my son shortly after his birth. It is poignant and full of truth. It shows a mother passing my baby son to my mother. All three are striking in appearance, but to see how my mother looked is devastating. It is how I remember her to be and yet she is unrecognisable from the photo of her holding me when I was only weeks old. Time and illness had completely ravaged her. Her face

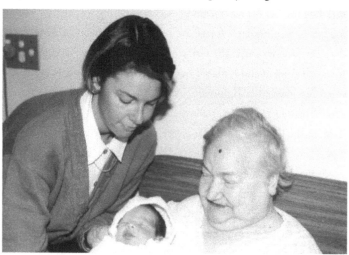

Three generations: Natalia, daughter-in-law Gena and grandson Simon, eight days old.

is soft and pudgy. The pudginess produces narrow slits for her eyes, a straight dentureless mouth, sagging jowls and a double chin. It is the ruined face of a ruined life.

I have been so critical of Natalia, my mother, that it makes me feel bad. Does she have any redeeming qualities at all? Does she leave any sort of legacy, is there a message one can grasp, a meaning that can be gleaned, that is in any way positive? The answer is yes. Natalia made me stronger; self-reliant and durable enough to survive life's troughs. There have been many times when I have had to call on those attributes to get through and I have always said a little thank you to my mother when I have.

For me, her message and the message of all those that have suffered beyond their measure, is simple. It does not require volumes to expound or tertiary degrees to understand. It is to savour life, every tasty morsel, as much and for as long as possible.